NatWest Small Business Bookshelf

This series has been written by a team of authors who all have many years' experience and are still actively involved in the day-to-day problems of the small business.

If you are running a small business or are thinking of setting up your own business, you have no time for the general, theoretical and often inessential detail of many business and management books. You need practical, readily accessible, easy-to-follow advice which relates to your own working environment and the problems you encounter. The books on the NatWest Small Business Bookshelf fulfil these needs.

- They concentrate on specific areas which are particularly problematic to the small business.

- They adopt a step-by-step approach to the implementation of sound business skills.

- They offer practical advice on how to tackle problems.

GW00326479

The author

William Lovell is an ex-HM Customs and Excise officer and has considerable experience with small businesses as a Visiting Officer as well as being an Adviser and Instructor on VAT from the early days of its introduction.

IMPORTANT NOTE – BUDGET 1991

- From 1 April 1991 a new VAT rate of 17.5 per cent will apply.

- The turnover limit for registration also increased to £35,000, the limit for deregistration being £33,600.

- The limit for bad debt relief has been reduced from two years to one year.

- The cash accounting scheme turnover limit has increased to £300,000.

NatWest Small Business Bookshelf

Understanding VAT

William Lovell

Pitman Publishing
128 Long Acre, London WC2E 9AN
A Division of Longman Group Limited

First published in Great Britain in association with the National Westminster Bank,
1990
Reissued in NatWest Business Handbooks series, 1991
Reprinted 1993, 1994

© Longman Group UK Ltd 1990

A CIP catalogue record for this book is available from the British Library

ISBN 0 273 03622 X

*The information in this book is intended as a general guide based upon the
legislation at the time of going to press. Neither the Bank, its staff or the author
can accept liability for any loss arising as a result of reliance upon any
information contained herein and readers are strongly advised to obtain
professional advice on an individual basis.*

Printed and bound in Singapore

Contents

Preface

The Vatman has, to date, issued 137 notices and leaflets about various aspects of VAT, with a couple dozen amendments and regular VAT notes, and is forever rewriting old leaflets and issuing new ones. The understandability factor of this load of literature is variable, and the reasons behind some of the instructions are often absent or, at best, inadequate.

This book is not a list of liabilities, i.e. which goods and services are taxable at what rates, and could never hope to be: to find out what the Vatman sees as the liability of a supply of goods or services, you must refer to his publications. What follows is intended to make the *administration* of VAT less of a burden to the smaller business – the one-man band, the husband and wife partnership, even the smaller limited companies: the sort of businesses which don't have a separate accounts office staffed by bookkeeping experts who do nothing else all day. And frankly, you'll be surprised how easy some of it can be.

If you find your way blocked, even after reading this book all the way through, don't sit there and make yourself ill over it . . . Call the Vatman (and have a witness to your call), or write to him (and keep a copy of the letter): if things have got to this point, you'll see why you need your own evidence when you come to the last chapter. Anyway, the best of luck and may you come up smiling.

William Lovell
January 1990

1 Introduction

How does VAT work? □ Exports □ 1992

VAT is *not* a tax on profits, turnover, dividends, gross mark-up, margins or anything else you can think of. It is not part of your business accounts at all . . . If you ignored VAT altogether, your trading figures would remain exactly the same. VAT *is* a tax on final consumer spending, collected in stages. Basically, if a customer spends £100 on your goods, he gives you an extra £15 for the government (with a VAT rate of 15 per cent) and, yes, you become an unpaid tax collector! Where do you find out all about VAT, what is taxable at what rate, what isn't taxable and so on? If you are approaching VAT for the first time (or even if you think you know it all after several years of it), you should get some of the Vatman's publications:

- Notice 700, the general guide.
- Leaflet 700/13, the list of notices and leaflets available (free) at all VAT offices.
- Leaflet 701/39, *VAT Liability Law*, which lists what is **zero-rated** and what is **exempt**.

You will have noticed that there is no list of what is taxable at **standard rate** – and there isn't one: if it doesn't appear in either the zero rate or exempt list, then it's taxable at standard rate, although there are a few exceptions.

How does VAT work?

An example

A prime producer supplies a cow hide and the final consumer buys a pair of boots. In between, the cow hide passes through various hands and various processes, *increasing in value* at each stage. Each person in the supply chain collects a sum of money from the next person down the line and deducts from it the tax he paid to the previous person, and the difference between what he paid and what he collected goes to the Vatman, as illustrated in Fig. 1.1.

	Buying price	Selling price	Paid to Vatman
Prime producer	—	£10 + 1	£1
Tanner	£10 + 1	£20 + 2	£1
Wholesaler	£20 + 2	£30 + 3	£1
Manufacturer	£30 + 3	£40 + 4	£1
Distributor	£40 + 4	£50 + 5	£1
Retailer	£50 + 5	£60 + 6	£1
Customer	£60 + 6	—	—

In this example, VAT has been taken at 10% for simplicity.

Fig. 1.1 Example of how VAT works

Why bother?

Suppose the distributor exported the boots – the Vatman would want to know how much to repay him for the VAT he had already paid. And suppose the retailer decamps with the money – at least the Vatman has collected £5, so it is not a complete loss.

Overheads

All business expenses are included, not just stock in trade. Each trader in the supply chain adds up all the VAT he has collected on his sales and subtracts from it all the VAT he has paid out on goods *and* running expenses, like accountancy bills, till rolls, cleaning, repairs, showcases, bill heads – everything.

Services

It is just the same for services, although there is usually no 'supply chain': your accountant, for instance, has expenses on which he pays VAT, but he creates his services himself, adds VAT to his price, subtracts his expenses VAT and gives the difference to the Vatman.

The VAT 'ring'

But suppose you don't sell to the final consumer: surely all you are doing is helping a lump of money go round in a circle, getting nowhere and doing nothing. After all, what you collect and pay to the Vatman, your customer claims back from the Vatman . . . Yes, it sometimes looks like that, especially in a group of companies where, perhaps, a service company makes supplies only to its associated companies and doesn't trade with the outside market at all. Sorry, but that is the system – if you are in business, you have to join the club. But there are ways of avoiding the money-go-round among associated companies (see 'Growing' in Chapter 2).

Refunds

But what happens if you spend more on VAT on your purchases than you collect on your sales? Don't fret – it happens quite often, especially if you deal in zero rate goods or exports, or you have sudden expenses (like replacing expensive machinery, stocking up for Christmas, etc.), or if you are just starting in business and have high setting-up costs. Provided you have done nothing illegal, *the Vatman will pay you*. And that, really, is how VAT works: subtract VAT on purchases from VAT on sales and pay the difference to the Vatman; if VAT on purchases is greater than VAT on sales, the Vatman pays the difference to you.

'VAT on purchases' and 'VAT on sales' are cumbersome expressions. From here on, it will make things much simpler if the Vatman's own terms and expressions are used: it is so much easier if both sides use the same jargon. I have met people who steadfastly refused to use the Vatman's terms and invented their own. In every case, they confused themselves and got their figures wrong, which annoyed the Vatman, who then issued assessments for the missing tax.

Glossary

consideration. The money or money's worth given in exchange for a supply of goods or services; for example, '5p off' vouchers, green stamps, or the old goods traded in for the new are all money's worth.

exempt. Supplies which are neither standard nor zero rate. The significance is that, in theory, input tax relating to exempt outputs cannot be recovered.

goods. Apart from the obvious goods like a bar of chocolate, nuts and bolts, a car or an ocean liner, other less obvious things are classed as goods; for example, heat, light, power, ventilation and refrigeration. The hiring out of equipment to provide any of these is a supply of services. A 'major interest' in land and buildings is goods, but rights over land are services.

input tax, output tax. Obviously the tax chargeable on inputs or outputs. Since purchase tax was abolished, and in Britain we have no sales tax, turnover tax or anything similar, the Vatman invented the terms 'input tax' and 'output tax' to identify where VAT is paid or collected by a business.

inputs. Goods or services coming in to the business, i.e. goods and services you have paid for.

LVO. The Local VAT Office, where the Vatman mostly works. Always make your first enquiries at the LVO.

net tax. The difference between input tax and output tax; either payable to the Vatman or repayable to the business.

notification. The act of telling the Vatman that you should be registered (unless you can claim exemption). But, once you reach the notification level of trade, you must notify.

outputs. Goods or services going out of the business, i.e. what you sell.

outside the scope of VAT. Some goods and services may be neither taxable nor exempt, even though made by a taxable person; for example, supplies made outside the country or not in the course of business. Supplies made by an unregistered person, even in the course of business, are outside the scope of VAT; so are all licences and statutory charges.

services. Anything done for a consideration which is *not* a supply of goods is a supply of services. Apart from obvious services like those of an accountant or solicitor, these include: the hire of goods in most cases, repairs of all kinds, making up another person's goods, hire of staff, assignment of rights (copyright, patents rights, use of a trade name, etc.). Even *not* doing something for a consideration is a service. The test is: has ownership of goods changed? If not, it is services.

standard rate. The positive rate of VAT charged on taxable supplies – currently 15 per cent.

supply. Everything you deal in is a supply, whether it is goods or services, taxable, zero rate or exempt, or outside the scope of VAT.

taxable person. A trader who is, or should be, registered.

trader. Anyone who is in business of any kind – be it trade, profession or vocation. Simply the Vatman's shorthand for anyone other than a Vatman!

VAT fraction. The mathematical fraction applied to a tax-inclusive price to extract the amount of VAT included. It is:

$$\frac{\text{Rate of Tax}}{100 + \text{Rate of Tax}}$$

With a tax rate of 15 per cent, this becomes $\frac{15}{115} = \frac{3}{23}$

VAT 1. The registration form.

VAT 2. List of partners; goes with VAT 1.

VAT 100. The return of VAT.

VCU. The VAT Central Unit – one of the Vatman's headquarters offices, at Southend-on-Sea. The place where returns are sent and received and numbers are crunched. It is a computer with human support – do not try to make enquiries direct.

VSO. The VAT Sub-Office – a branch office which has no enquiries or correspondence facilities.

zero rate. Oddly enough, this is a rate of tax, although the rate is nil.

Loss or theft of goods

What about losses or theft? How is VAT handled in such cases? Take the case of a confectioner who buys £100 of ice-cream, pays his supplier, recovers the input tax from the Vatman and stacks the ice-cream in his freezer. There is a power failure, the freezer defrosts and all the confectioner can do is to bail out the freezer and pour the stuff down the drain. What does the Vatman do about the VAT? Nothing. Why? Because the ice-cream had not been *supplied*. It would be just the same if the ice-cream (or any other goods) had been stolen: there has been no legal supply, therefore there can be no tax on a supply. Everyone, including the Vatman, says, for instance: 'Ice-cream is taxable at the standard rate'. But, to be absolutely accurate, ice-cream is not taxable at the standard rate: it is the *supply* of ice-cream that is taxable at the standard rate.

On the shelf

In the days of purchase tax, the tax was stuck on the goods at the manufacture/import stage and stayed with them all the way through to the final consumer. If the goods were lost, stolen or destroyed, the purchase tax paid by the trader was lost and he had a lot of trouble getting it back. Usually, his insurance company had to pay up. But, under VAT, goods on the shelf are tax-free, and the tax becomes chargeable only when they are supplied. Think how difficult it would be to hold services, 'on the shelf', tax-paid!

Thus, VAT is a transaction tax, if you like to think of it that way, charged only when a transaction takes place, and if goods are lost, stolen or destroyed, there has been no legal transaction on which VAT could be charged.

Theft of money

But what happens when goods or services have been supplied and paid for, and the money is stolen? The Vatman will call for the tax, because there has been a supply. The loss of cash, like the loss of goods, should be made good by the insurance company.

There will be no further reference to tax on a supply. If you remember that VAT is chargeable on these goods, or those services, you won't go far wrong.

Exempt *v.* zero rate

What exactly is the difference between the two? They both mean 'no tax', don't they? Not quite. A person who deals only in exempt supplies (see Leaflet 701/39 Sch. 6) cannot register and so cannot recover any input tax charged to him. An undertaker, for instance, is charged VAT on all his expenses, including the coffin, furniture and fittings, and the only way to recover it is to include it in the price of the funeral, which is 'exempt'. Thus, there is always an element of VAT concealed within an exempt supply. However, a person who deals in zero rate supplies (see Sch. 5) can register for VAT and can, therefore, recover all his input tax; consequently, the goods or services he supplies are completely free of VAT.

Liability of a supply

The liability of a supply means, simply, whether the supply is taxable (at standard or zero rate), or exempt. When VAT was first introduced, this was easy to decide: you looked in the zero or exempt schedules to see what, obviously, was zero-rated or exempt, and if it wasn't there, it was standard rate. Thus, the liability depended upon the *nature of the supply, not on the status of the customer.* There were a few exceptions – like diplomats and visiting forces, under the Vienna Convention – and that was all. (And in any case, any diplomat entitled to relief from VAT paid it in the first place and then applied to the Foreign and Commonwealth Office for a refund.) However, there were plenty of local purchasing officers in the armed forces who had rubber stamps made up to the effect that 'We don't pay VAT', which they plastered all over local traders' invoices. This caused no end of trouble – which could be sorted out only at ministry level, in Whitehall!

Relief

Take my word for it: everyone pays VAT, from the Queen down to the single-parent family on state benefit, including the armed forces, government departments, health authorities, local authorities, charities, schools, doctors, the butcher, the baker, the candlestick maker. *Everybody*. So, if someone comes along and says 'We don't pay VAT', demand that he quotes the law that says so, and to produce an order signed by his Commanding Officer, Head of Department, Managing Director, *quoting the section of the law*, and still don't believe him until you've checked with your LVO.

Exceptions

There are some exceptions – dipomats and visiting forces have already been mentioned – and there are certain situations where normally standard rate supplies can be made at zero rate, provided the rules are learned first. It's not advisable trying to get the liability changed after the supply has been made and paid for. (See Leaflet 701/1, *Gifts to Charity*; 701/6, *Donated Medical Equipment*; 701/7, *Aids for the Handicapped*.) These were fairly restricted and specialised circumstances, and, of course, there are always exports (see Chapter 7). However, the field of customer-status-related liability has now been opened up by the European Court to take in many supplies to a business, registered or not, in the fields of land, buildings and construction (see Notice 742 and Leaflets 708/1, 2, 3); fuel and power (see Leaflet 701/19); water and sewerage (see Leaflet 701/16). Supplies to domestic consumers or to charities for non-business purposes will remain zero-rated. And, thanks to the EC, there may be more of these in the future.

So now, if someone comes to you and says 'We are entitled to zero-rating' – not all the same thing as 'We don't pay VAT' – you will have to get from him a certificate of entitlement, stating that he is, indeed, entitled to zero-rating, in a form laid down by the Vatman in the notices and leaflets on the particular supply. And if he gives you a false certificate, the Vatman goes after him for the tax! (See Chapter 5.)

Consideration

Why does the Vatman refer to 'consideration'? Is it just bureaucratic gobbledegook, using highfalutin jargon instead of a simple word like 'price' or 'value' or 'cash'? There is a reason. The Vatman wants the tax on the *value* of the supply, no matter how it is paid for. A voucher offering you '5p off your next purchase of Sudso', trading checks, green stamps, petrol tokens, the value of the traded-in van or office typewriter are all *money's worth*, and the Vatman wants 15 per cent of the value. Even on a barter deal. This is quite common in the oil industry, where, if one company runs out of a particular product, it will arrange for a 'competitor' to supply its customers, and replace the product later with an equivalent supply. The Vatman still wants 15 per cent of the value of the supplies. So don't think you can swap gardening services for a bit of accountancy, or free financial advice for a new office block: the Vatman will find out sooner or later, and when he demands his 15 per cent, you'll have a tough time refusing him!

Exports

So far, it has been assumed that you are trading solely on the home market – all your customers are UK residents. But what about exports, foreign tourists, overseas customers?

Export of goods

The export of goods is relatively simple: provided you control the export and can produce the necessary documents to the Vatman – and can prove that the goods were in fact exported – you don't charge VAT. Exports will be dealt with more fully in Chapter 7, but for now, remember that *you* must control the export: you cannot 'zero-rate' a supply to someone else in the UK because you 'know' that he is going to export it.

Export of services

The export of services is not so straightforward: basically you must be able to show that the 'principal beneficiary' of your services is outside the UK (see Leaflet 701/39, Sch. 5, Group 11 and Notice 741). This also will be dealt with in more detail later.

Overseas customers

When it comes to 'foreign' customers, there are two distinct classes: those from inside the EC, and the rest of the world. Currently, customers within the EC *may* have to be charged VAT on some goods and services, while the 'rest' get it tax-free.

Retail exports

There might be visitors and tourists, who, not too surprisingly, will object to paying VAT on goods they are taking out of the country, and even on goods and services they consume within the country! There is a 'retail export scheme' you can operate if you wish, but you are responsible for the VAT! And visitors get no relief on supplies consumed within the UK.

1992

This, then, has been a quick gallop through the 'how' of VAT: everything is contained within the borders of the UK, and VAT incurred in other member states of the EC cannot be claimed through UK VAT structures, but only by applying to the Ministry of Finance in the other state (see Notice 723). But come 1992, all remaining restrictions between member states are supposed to disappear, after which you are supposed to be able to reclaim, through your UK VAT return, any VAT incurred in another state *and* you will charge full-rate VAT to all EC customers, visitors, and travellers, whatever their business or status. At the time of writing, there has been no hint on how this is to be achieved, not least because – believe it or not – there are at least two different systems of VAT in use in the EC! (See Fig. 1.2.)

When VAT was introduced, there was the choice of getting rid of all other taxes and duties and having a multiple rate VAT system, under which not all input tax was deductible, there was no exempt class and very little zero-rating. Or, excise duties could be left where they were, with VAT being charged on top, with zero-rating and exemptions. Guess which system Britain adopted? Yes, the second alternative. And Ireland's VAT is calculated on a tax-inclusive price!

10 Understanding VAT

Belgium	Rate %	0	6	17	19	25	33
	Fraction	—	$\frac{3}{53}$	$\frac{17}{117}$	$\frac{19}{119}$	$\frac{1}{5}$	$\frac{1}{4}$
Britain	Rate %	0	15				
	Fraction	—	$\frac{3}{23}$				
Denmark	Rate %	0	22				
	Fraction	—	$\frac{11}{61}$				
France	Rate %	5.5	7	18.6	33		
	Fraction	$\frac{11}{211}$	$\frac{7}{107}$	$\frac{93}{500}$	$\frac{1}{4}$		
Germany	Rate %	7	14				
	Fraction	$\frac{7}{107}$	$\frac{14}{57}$				
Greece	Rate %	6	18	36			
	Fraction	$\frac{3}{53}$	$\frac{9}{59}$	$\frac{9}{34}$			
Holland	Rate %	6	20				
	Fraction	$\frac{3}{53}$	$\frac{1}{6}$				
Ireland	Rate %	0	10	25	(These are tax-inclusive rates)		
	Fraction	—	—	—			
Italy	Rate %	4	9	19	38		
	Fraction	$\frac{1}{26}$	$\frac{9}{109}$	$\frac{19}{119}$	$\frac{19}{69}$		
Luxemburg	Rate %	3	6	12			
	Fraction	$\frac{3}{103}$	$\frac{3}{53}$	$\frac{3}{28}$			
Portugal	Rate %	0	6	8	12	16	21	30
	Fraction	—	$\frac{3}{53}$	$\frac{2}{27}$	$\frac{3}{28}$	$\frac{4}{29}$	$\frac{21}{121}$	$\frac{3}{13}$
Spain	Rate %	0	6	12	33		
	Fraction	—	$\frac{3}{53}$	$\frac{3}{28}$	$\frac{1}{4}$		

Fig. 1.2 VAT rates and fractions in use in the EC

2 How do I register?

Are you in business? □ When to register □ Exemption from registration □ Staying registered – or not □ The who and the how of registration □ After registration □ Miscellany

Since most people register only once, it's worth taking a bit of trouble to get it right the first time: after all, once you're registered, you can claim back all the VAT you've paid out on all manner of goods and expenses . . . Well – not quite. There are conditions to being registered, sometimes to your advantage, sometimes to the Vatman's. For instance, he can insist on your being registered, even if you don't want to be; or he can make assessments for tax and penalties if you get it wrong or don't do it at the right time; or even refuse to register you.

For a start, you will need to get the notices and leaflets listed below from your LVO (you will find the address in the telephone directory under 'Customs and Excise Department' or 'VAT', depending on the whim of the local collector). These notices contain the Vatman's view of things – which is what matters! And they are free.

- Notice 700, *The VAT Guide* – the basic reference book on VAT.
- Leaflet 700/1, *Should I Be Registered for VAT?* – a list of questions and answers which, although the Vatman thinks it answers the question in the title, does not go nearly far enough.
- Leaflet 700/13 or 13A – a list of VAT publications updated twice a year, hence the 13A alternative, identifying all of the Vatman's notices and leaflets in *numerical order of publication*. You will have to go through the whole list, looking for anything that has any bearing on your business.
- Leaflet 701/39 *VAT, Liability Law* – not as forbidding as it looks: it is merely a reprint of Schs. 5 – 6 of the VAT Act 1983, listing what is zero-rated and what is exempt. If you can't find what you're looking for in either list, it's standard rate, and you are potentially registrable. If what you do is only in the exempt schedule, stop reading here: you cannot register. If you have a mixture of standard and zero rate and exempt, keep reading, because your level of standard and zero-rate outputs, i.e. your *taxable* supplies, will determine whether you should register.

Are you in business?

There is no legal definition of 'business', so the Vatman will look at what you are doing and decide whether you are *making business supplies*. It doesn't matter how low your turnover is – if you want to be registered, the Vatman cannot refuse to register you, provided you are making, or can show that you intend to make, supplies in the course of business. You no longer have to prove that you are making a living at it – just that it is *business:* it is not for the Vatman to decide whether you have a successful business, are running at a loss, or haven't a clue. If you insist on being registered, he cannot refuse. However, once you're registered, you're *in* – so look at Chapters 3 and 8 before you insist too strongly!

Two cautionary tales

1. The VAT 1 said that the business was a squash club, but the turnover quoted was clearly too little to allow for any sort of commercial operation once you considered the cost of just running the place. Further enquiries revealed that a bunch of friends, unable to book a good regular game of squash, decided to build their own squash court and thought they could register while they built it, get all the VAT back on materials (they planned a DIY effort) and then deregister. The Registration Senior Officer decided that the operation was not a business and refused registration.
2. A couple applied to register in advance of making taxable supplies while converting a trawler to a pleasure craft – a perfectly legal procedure – and, naturally, they wanted to recover their VAT as they went along (and when the conversion was complete, the supply would be well over the registration limit). However, enquiries revealed that they had a string of failed businesses behind them, some registered, some not, at several LVOs, and the Registration Senior Officer refused registration on the grounds that he was not satisfied that they intended to make taxable supplies, or were even capable of doing so. They could not even produce a prospective buyer and were quite capable of sailing away with the boat . . . and the Vatman's money.

Extreme cases, no doubt, but they illustrate the point that you must be, or can demonstrate that you will be, *making business supplies*, not just following a hobby or pastime, and not perhaps thinking of possibly making a supply at some vague time in the future. Furthermore, those supplies have to be *taxable* supplies; so, if you do a bit of standard rate, a bit of zero rate and a bit of exempt, the exempt is ignored for the purpose of deciding whether you should be registered, and only the combined level of standard and zero rate outputs will be considered. From here on, whenever taxable supplies are mentioned, you should always take it to mean standard *and* zero rate.

When to register

Notification

The Vatman requires you to tell him when you are liable to be registered. This procedure is called: **notification**. And it is a warning that cannot be too often repeated: *you must notify at the right time.*

It is to be supposed that you are conducting a business you know something about and that you have taken appropriate advice from an accountant, solicitor, trade association, and the like. Obviously, you will be in business to make money, so you will keep a running check on how the business is doing, or you will calculate what you expect the turnover to be. Then, depending on how much money you pull in, there are *specific dates* on which you must notify the Vatman of your turnover. There may, in fact, be reasons why you need not register, or you may be able to claim special exemption from registration, but you must notify first and argue about non-registration after. *When* must you notify? When you reach the registration limit.

Registration limit (see Appendix)

The registration limit is the annual turnover at which you must notify: at the time of writing, it is £23,600 per year, and is usually increased a few hundred pounds in the Budget each year, more or less in line with inflation. However, if you reach a turnover of £8,000 in a calendar quarter, you must notify then. If your arithmetic is any good, you will have spotted that £8,000 per quarter is £32,000 per year – rather more than the registration limit of only £23,600 a year. There is a reason: business is never dead level and even; it goes up and down seasonally, or with inflation, or due to entirely local factors, and if, taking all that into account, you reach £8,000 in a quarter, you are virtually certain to exceed the annual registration limit, and it therefore makes a difference as to *when* to notify. As you watch the registration limit creep up each year, remember that the quarterly limit will be about one-third of the annual figure. Let us put one myth to death here and now: the registration limit is not the amount of money you can earn before you have to register. You do not have a year's trading free of the Vatman before you need to register!

Gradual build-up of business (see Appendix)

You must keep a regular check on your takings, week by week, month by month, quarter by quarter. It makes no difference what your business is – corner shop, budding author, fashion photographer, motor mechanic, actor, anything: you must keep a check on your takings. Then, on the quarter dates of March 31, June 30, September 30 and December 31, you must see whether you have taken £8,000 or more in the previous calendar quarter. It does not matter what financial year you have chosen, or when you opened for business the first time – you must use these dates. And you cannot ignore a less-than-3-months' period if you exceeded the £8,000 limit between starting date and the first quarter date. But you do not have to calculate a pro-rata turnover figure to see if you would have exceeded the £8,000 in a full quarter. The test is: have you exceeded the quarterly limit on one of these dates? If you have, then you must *notify within 30 days* – that is, by April 30, July 30, October 30 or January 30. Then, if you are required to be registered, you will be registered as from May 1, August 1, November 1 or February 1. But suppose you have not exceeded the quarterly limit on any of these dates . . . Have you exceeded the annual limit in the previous four quarters? If so, you must still notify, using the same notification dates, and *it is the previous four quarters that count*, not the previous calendar year.

If you are late in notifying, the Vatman will assess you for a penalty (the procedure is quite automatic and takes no notice of knowledge or lack of it, or lack of fraudulent intent) based on your presumed net tax for the number of days late: 10 per cent of the net tax up to nine months late; 20 per cent up to 18 months late; and 30 per cent over 18 months. Plus interest on the withheld tax, all subject to a minimum penalty of £50.

All zero rate outputs

Obviously, in this case you are not withholding tax, *but you must still notify*; those zero-rated supplies might change to standard rate at any time, and if you are not registered, or not specially exempted from registration, you could get a nasty surprise when the Vatman catches up with you.

Seasonal trade (see Appendix)

What if you exceed the quarterly limit in one or two quarters of the year, but close down for the off season and never reach the annual limit? Quite simply, the Vatman doesn't want to know — he's got enough to do, dealing with the 1,250,000 traders who are registered! However, if you *do not* close down, and you exceed the limit in one quarter, you must notify: there is always the chance that you will exceed the annual limit, and if you did not notify at the right time, the Vatman can backtrack to the point where you should have notified, register you from then, and collect back tax, penalties and interest.

Two cautionary tales

1. A trader was advised by his accountant that *that* trade in *that* location would never reach the registration limit, so when he went over the quarterly limit in his first quarter's trading, he put it down to seasonal fluctuation and did not notify. When he went over the limit again in the next quarter, he realised that his accountant knew less about trade than he did about accounting, and decided he'd better notify. Which he did, and the Vatman backdated his registration to the end of the first quarter.

2. On the other hand, there was the Bed & Breakfast operator who had been plugging along for years, trading only in the season, who suddenly found himself catering for a construction gang in the off season, and galloping over the registration limit. He notified in the proper manner and asked to be exempted from registration because he could show that his pattern of trade was such that he never normally exceeded the limit, would never be trading in the off season again and would certainly not make the limit in the *next* four quarters. The Vatman agreed that he need not be registered.

Take-over (see Appendix)

If you are taking over an existing business which is, or *should* be, registered, notify the Vatman at once — as soon as you know the date on which you will take over: that will be your registration date. But, *should* be registered? Oh, yes – suppose you are buying one of a string of shops, each of which trades above the minimum level, but have all been included within a single registration. Or part of a holiday complex, a hived-off factory, a franchise operation or something of the sort, which, *in its own right*, has a turnover above the limit: you must notify the Vatman of the date on which you will take over, and become responsible for the VAT affairs of the business. Late notification, even if the correct date is notified and registration is backdated to the correct date, still attracts a penalty. (See Leaflet 700/9.)

Future success (see Appendix)

If you are setting up a business, but are not yet trading (i.e. you become, in the Vatman's jargon, an 'intending trader'), not only will you want to be registered to avoid penalties, you will also want to recover your input tax as you go along, to help finance the setting-up of the business – like the couple with the trawler. You could be preparing to open a shop in a new development and want to be ready on ceremonial opening day. Or developing a new housing or industrial estate, but where no one will be moving in for several months (at least). Or about to burst on the market with a new invention that will sweep the board! All expensive operations, in terms of getting in stock and capital equipment, sub-contractors, materials, development costs, etc. – all of which carry VAT.

Obviously, your notification/registration date becomes a bit hazy. You would therefore discuss things with the Vatman – despite the rumours, he's really quite human (and some of him are hers) – and quite naturally, he will want to know the date on which you expect to make your first supply. It's no good saying, 'Well, I'm going to start trading – sometime'. He will simply put your application in the LBW (Let the Blighter Wait!) file. You will have to produce some tangible evidence of your intention to trade: the lease of the shop and orders/quotations for filling the shelves; rights to a building site and planning permission to develop it; orders from prospective customers. *Something*. You can't do what one potential 'builder' tried to do: he offered to supply a sworn affidavit that he intended to trade! But he had no tangible evidence of his intention to trade, so he was not registered.

The Vatman may then agree to register you as an intending trader. But remember: intending registration is at the discretion of the Registration Officer. If you can't convince him that you really will trade, there's nothing you can do about it, unless you are prepared to go to a VAT tribunal and listen to the Vatman explain why he considers you an unhealthy risk to the revenue.

After all this – when is your registration date? I have said that the Vatman is quite reasonable, so fix on a mutually acceptable date, preferably the first day of a month, and no more than a year ahead of your first expected supply: although the Vatman cannot refuse to register you, an application too far in advance of the first day of trading may persuade him that you do not, after all, intend to trade.

Voluntary registration

Perhaps you have been plugging along, doing all right but no great shakes, below the registration limit, and you recognise that you will never get much further unless you can compete with registered traders – after all, the only way you can recover your input tax is to include it in your selling price. But does that matter? Registered traders stick VAT on to their prices, don't they? Ah, yes – but they can give tax invoices which allow other registered traders to claim input tax, and if they are dealing in zero-rated supplies, there will be no hidden tax, as there is with you.

In some cases, you can't get within sniffing distance of a more lucrative market unless you are registered. Some big traders simply will not take on an unregistered sub-contractor, and even pupil barristers can't take their first brief until they are registered. It can be quite an advantage to be registered: there is nothing in the registration number to show that it is a voluntary registration, so it immediately looks as though you have a greater turnover than is perhaps the case! And customers, trade or private, often prefer a larger trader to an obviously struggling one.

So – what is your notification/registration date? Discuss it with the Vatman. It will obviously be a current date. You should choose the first day of a month for convenience. But remember: you will have to be making *business supplies*, not conducting a hobby and doing favours for friends. You can be both voluntary and intending – but be prepared to convince the Vatman, especially if your turnover is very low.

Summary

- Build-up: you must notify not later than January 30, April 30, July 30 or October 30, if you exceeded the quarterly limit in the previous three months, or the annual limit in the previous four calendar quarters.
- Take-over: notify as soon as you know the date on which you will take over, so that registration can be effective from the actual take-over date.
- Intending trader: notify one year ahead of your first expected sale.
- Voluntary: the notification date is any mutually agreeable current date. If you wish to register earlier than the legally required date in order, for instance, to recover tax on purchases and other expenditure, you should consider intending and/or voluntary status.

Exemption from registration

It is a warning that cannot be too often repeated: once you have reached that magical quarterly or annual limit, you must notify. However, notification is not always followed by registration: you can apply to be specially exempted from registration, but there are only three situations where this is possible:

1. **Seasonal.** You are a seasonal trader, and although you have exceeded the limit in one or two quarters, you will not reach the annual limit because of reduced trade in the off season. If you close down for the off season and never come within sight of the annual limit, the Vatman doesn't want to know. But, if you trade all year round, but never make the annual limit despite a couple of goods quarters, you must notify and explain why you wish to be exempted from registration, backing up your claim with facts and figures from previous seasons.

2. **Exceptional.** Although you have exceeded the limit now, it was because of exceptional conditions, which will never happen again, and you will not make the annual limit in the next four calendar quarters. Like the Bed & Breakfast operator who was landed with a construction gang in the off season.

3. **Zero rate.** All your outputs are zero rate and you can see no profit in having to fill in a VAT return every three months and have the Vatman come nosing round your business. This needs

careful consideration. All your outputs may be zero rate, but what about inputs? There will be the VAT on petrol, accountant, repairs, renewals, telephone, etc., and if you have been granted exemption from registration, *there is no way* you can get that VAT back, no matter what the circumstances.

I would not recommend exemption on zero-rating alone, unless your inputs are really very small. And what if you have a small amount of standard rate sales, like the butcher who sells Christmas trees once a year? The Vatman may still consider granting exemption; but suppose your standard rate sales were a business purchase by a registered trader – say, for business gifts – and you could not give a tax invoice.

Not only would you lose that sale, but if word got around that you weren't big enough to be registered, it could affect the rest of your trade. Therefore, even if your outputs are all zero rate, you must still notify, and then argue about exemption. In a nutshell: notify first, argue after!

Staying registered – or not

Suppose, for whatever reason, you do not want to remain registered, even though you are continuing in business: is there any way out? In fact, there is no legal bar to your requesting deregistration at any time, and if the business collapses, or never gets going, the Vatman will not insist on your remaining registered, just out of plain cussedness. However, you will not be allowed to dodge in and out of registration as your turnover fluctuates or as circumstances suit you, especially if you have claimed tax back from the Vatman. This point will be discussed later, but, if you claim back tax on purchases when you register, you have to declare tax on stocks when you cancel!

Yo-yo (see Appendix)

And don't think you can notify when your turnover goes over the quarterly limit, plead seasonal fluctuation, claim exemption, and then do it again and again. Don't forget, the Vatman has a computer which will soon pinpoint anyone trying that!

Fragmentation

Also, don't think you can avoid registration by splitting up the business among the family, each of them trading below the limit:

the Vatman can deem a fragmented business to be a single business, register it from a date of his choosing, and get busy with assessments, penalties and even prosecution. Like the fish and chip shop that was run by father on Monday, mother on Tuesday, daughter on Wednesday, son on Thursday, a couple of them on Friday, a different pair on Saturday and everyone on Sunday. Or the shoe shop, where each fitting stool was a separate business. Or the hairdresser, where each chair was a separate business. The Vatman decided that each of these was in fact a single business and registered each one, with penalties, from a date of his choosing.

Separate business

But what about genuinely separate businesses like, say, husband and wife, each an accountant working from home, each with their own circle of clients? It would be too much to expect that if one of *her* clients phoned up, *he* would refuse to speak to them – there might be only the one telephone, anyway. Provided that the businesses are genuinely separate, with separate accounts and bank accounts, and a separate client list, the Vatman may allow separate registration – or even allow them to continue below the registration limit. But he would need convincing! Why couldn't those others be treated as separate businesses? Not least because there was no way any one of them could claim to have a separate circle of customers, and they used common stock and common equipment, even if they did have artificially separate accounts.

Mixed business

Standard rate, zero rate, exempt – it is quite easy for one business to have all three. Plus 'outside the scope'! Like a builder with zero rate domestic building, standard rate repairs and commercial building, exempt rights over land, and outside the scope selling imported materials on the high seas! Accountants and solicitors commonly draw exempt commission from finance and insurance companies, building societies and client bank accounts. So just because your principal business is standard rate, don't assume that all the side lines are as well. Especially don't think that, if your principal supplies are zero rate, everything else is too. Nor should you assume that you can recover all input tax, either. So do plough through Leaflet 700/13 to see if there is anything that applies to you.

Other income

It has been stressed that it is your *taxable* turnover that decides whether you should be registered – but you could still have other income, either exempt (see Chapter 5) or outside the scope of VAT. This is not an easy concept to grasp, particularly if the other income is a result of business activities conducted outside the country – like the builder selling imported goods on the high seas, i.e. before it is landed in the UK. Or what about the pillar of the local business society who gets elected to the Council or some other public position, which pays him something, if only expenses: is that income taxable or not? It will depend on whether he obtains the position as part of his business activities – in which case, it is part of his taxable business – or because of his personal reputation. Election to the Council is definitely not part of his business. Nor his appointment as Hon. Treasurer of the Cricket Club because he plays a good, straight bat and in business is an accountant, and so is an ideal person for such a position. But his appointment as adviser to a local Preservation Society, for instance, because of his legal knowledge and standing, would be part of the business. (But see the distinction between 'sole proprietor' and 'partnership' below.)

However, be of good cheer! Most of the time, it will be perfectly obvious whether what you are doing is taxable business or not, and these odds and ends are mentioned only to make you aware that they can crop up, and if some once-in-a-blue-moon situation does crop up, don't worry about it: get a written explanation from the Vatman.

The who and the how of registration

In the last section, great play was made of notification, and you may have guessed that merely writing or telephoning to the Vatman is not enough: there is a form to be filled in. Of course, you will have to write or telephone to get the form, and since the Vatman keeps a record of such requests, he may well come back to you to find out why he hasn't had the form back. The form is the VAT 1, and with it should come:

- Notice 700.
- Notice 41 (list of trade classifications).
- Form VAT 2 (list of partners).
- Possibly a local questionnaire and perhaps a few other things he may think useful.

And if you haven't already got them, you should ask for Leaflets 700/13 and 701/39.

Accountants often keep a stock of VAT 1's, but the form changes from time to time, and a notification on the wrong form is not a legal notification. Nor will your accountant have a stock of the official notices and leaflets. And it will be not the slightest use pleading that you didn't know this or that — VAT has been going since 1973 and there simply cannot be anyone in the country unaware of it, or not knowing that there is a whole gang of civil servants charged with administering it. So get the Vatman's own publications and at least read the table of contents — ignorance of the law will not be accepted as a 'reasonable excuse'.

Filling in the form

The best way to decide what goes in each of the 16 items of the Form VAT 1 is to work through them, one by one, but not necessarily in the order in which they appear on the form. But first, a general comment on the actual filling in. As illustrated in Fig. 2.1, the VAT 1 is a computer input form and most of the items are divided up into little boxes requiring one letter or figure or space per box. Always start at the extreme left edge and take a little trouble over it: remember that a computer is a tin idiot and must have its information fed in in precisely the right way, and if you think you can't be bothered with nit-picking requirements, you'll only have yourself to blame if your repayments go astray or you get penalised for not notifying at the right time because your VAT 1 was unreadable.

Item 4 (Status of business)

This is the first to be considered and relates to the status of the person being registered. The choices are:

- *Sole proprietor.* The typical one-man band, doing everything — the work, the books, ordering, invoicing: shopkeeper, solicitor, farmer, designer, photographer, haulage contractor, artist, author — anything. There are two things to remember: 1. Anything a sole proprietor does counts towards his registered business and must be included in his VAT figures. You have not, for instance, registered a greengrocer's shop, you have registered *yourself* and declared your principal business to be a greengrocer's shop. So you can't do a bit of light haulage at weekends in your

VALUE ADDED TAX

Application for Registration

HM Customs and Excise

SPECIMEN

For official use

Date of receipt | 1

Local office code and registration number

Name

Trade name

Taxable turnover | EDR | D M Y | Stagger | Status

Rept. | Vol. | Oversize name address | Computer user | Group Div. | Intg. | Overseas

Bn | D M Y

You should open up this form and read the notes before you answer these questions. Please write clearly in ink.

Applicant and business

1 Full name

2 Trading name

3 Address

Phone no.

Postcode

4 Status of business

Limited company ☐ Company incorporation certificate no. and date day month year 19

Sole proprietor ☐ Partnership ☐ Other-specify

5 Business activity — Trade classification

6 Computer user ☐

Repayments of VAT

7 ☐ Bank sorting code and account no. — National Girobank account no.

VAT 1 — please continue overleaf →

Fig. 2.1 The VAT 1

(Reproduced with the permission of the Controller of Her Majesty's Stationery Office)

Compulsory registrations

8   Date of first taxable supply   day month year
        [   ] [   ] 19 [   ]   Value of taxable supplies in
                                          the 12 months from that date.   £ [   ]

9   Date from which you have to be registered   day month year
                                                         [   ] [   ] 19 [   ]

10 Exemption from compulsory registration   [   ]

        expected value of zero-rated supplies in the next 12 months   £ [   ]

Other types of registration

11 Taxable supplies below registration limits   [   ]

        value of taxable supplies in the last 12 months   £ [   ]

12 No taxable supplies made yet   [   ]

        (a)   expected annual value of taxable supplies   £ [   ]

        (b)   expected date of first taxable supply   day month year
                                                           [   ] [   ] 19 [   ]

Business changes and transfers

13 Business transferred as a going concern   [   ]

        (a)   date of transfer or change of legal status   day month year
                                                            [   ] [   ] 19 [   ]

        (b)   name of previous owner   [   ]

        (c)   previous VAT registration number (if known)   [   ]

14 Transfer of VAT registration number   [   ]

Related businesses

15 Other VAT registrations   Yes [   ]   No [   ]

Declaration – You must complete this declaration.

16 I _____

        (Full name in BLOCK LETTERS)

        declare that all the entered details and information in any accompanying documents are correct and complete.

        Signature _____   Date _____

        Proprietor [ ]   Partner [ ]   Director [ ]   Company Secretary [ ]   Authorised Official [ ]   Trustee [ ]

For official use

Registration	Obligatory	Exemption	Voluntary	Intending	Transfer of Regn. no.
Approved — Initial/Date					
Refused — Initial/Date					
Form Issued — Initial/Date	VAT 9/Other	VAT 8	VAT 7	Letter	Approval Letter

VAT 1 F3733(APRIL 1988)   Printed in the U K for H M S O   3/88 Dd 8120637 C 12500 38806 G1675

Fig. 2.1   (contd.)

greengrocer's van and exclude it from your business records.
2. When it comes to money troubles, a sole proprietor is *solely* responsible to the Vatman (and Payeman) for the tax – and they can take everything he's got, business and private, to satisfy the preferential debt to the Crown.

- *Partnership*. This can be a formal partnership, with a partnership agreement setting out the rights and responsibilities of each partner, how much each can take out of the business, even, perhaps, how much of the debts each is responsible for. Or it can be an informal partnership – most usually met when a husband and wife are running a shop, a farm, an accountancy practice, a hotel, etc. Each partner can then do his own thing on the side, separately from the partnership – even run an entirely separate business as a sole proprietor, or as a member of another partnership – provided that it is not a job obtained through the partnership. In the case of debts, the Vatman will normally pursue the *traceable* partner for all the tax owing by the partnership, and, as for the sole proprietor, not stopping short of personal property.
- *Limited company*. There are two sorts of limited company in Britain: the private limited company, identified by 'Ltd' after its name, and the public limited company, identified by 'plc' after its name and also known as a 'quoted' company, i.e. its shares are quoted on the Stock Exchange and anyone can buy them. Either sort of company is legally a person and can be treated in most instances like a real, live person. A limited company has a legal identity which is separate from its shareholders. Like an individual, the company itself can enter into contracts with other organisations and individuals, sue and be sued and prosecuted without involving its shareholders in the proceedings. Upon insolvency or liquidation, shareholders' liability is limited to the amount they have agreed to contribute to the company's debts. There are various other advantages to trading as a limited company (see *Starting Up* in this series), especially in the field of personal tax: consult your solicitor or accountant. Remember to enter the incorporation date of the company: registration *cannot* be earlier, unless you register as a partnership and later change your status.
- *Mixed status*. There is nothing to prevent a person from trading and being registered as a sole proprietor, as a partner in any number of partnerships (provided that there are different partners in each one) and as a director of any number of limited companies (even if, for instance, he and his wife are the only directors of

2

all of them). But you can register as a sole proprietor *only once*. (Don't forget the Vatman's attitude to fragmentation.)

- *Other*. There are various other categories that the Vatman will recognise, like non-profit-making organisations (I know, some businesses don't show a profit, but that's not what the Vatman means!) or a company limited by guarantee – neither of which is likely to interest the ordinary small trader. One 'other' that could crop up quite easily is the *unincorporated association*, i.e. any members' club (like the British Legion, sports and social clubs, old time dancing, shooting, bowling, angling clubs, etc.) that is run by an annually-elected committee. Such a club would be registered in its own name. (In the beginning, it had to be registered in the names of three committee members, and since they often changed every year, the Vatman soon got fed up with that!) Declarations are made by an 'authorised official' – invariably a committee member. A proprietor's club (like a night club, snooker hall, country club, etc.) would be registered as sole proprietor, partnership or limited company, as appropriate.

Item 1 (Full name) & Item 2 (Trading name)

These two clearly go together, and having decided on the status to appear in Item 4, you can now decide what name to register under.

- *Sole proprietor*. **Item 1** – your full, legal name (the one that appears on your birth, marriage or naturalisation certificate). You can add Mr, Mrs, Miss, the unpronounceable Ms, Sir, Lord, Dame, Earl, Countess, Colonel or Corporal – any rank or title you like, provided it is your legal identity. **Item 2** – if you trade under some other name, that other name must be entered here. If Ferdinand Dionysus Smith is better known as the pop singer Rock Granite, then Ferdinand etc. goes in Item 1 and Rock Granite in Item 2. If your shop, workshop or other business is known by some name different from your personal name, that different name must go in Item 2, e.g. Moreton-in-the-Marsh Kosher Take-away, Bolton Accessories, The Little Shop – whatever the trading name may be.
- *Partnership*. **Item 1** – this is not quite so straightforward, since Item 1 can be either the full names of the partners *or* the name of the partnership, but not the trading name, if this is something different again. This is best illustrated by the following examples: 1. No formal partnership name: the full names of all partners go in Item 1. This is most common with husband and wife (plus

son/daughter etc.) trading in informal partnership. 2. Formal partnership with a name different from that of the partners. The partnership name goes in Item 1. You have surely come across a firm of solicitors or accountants with a name like Grants or Johnson & Johnson, with never a Grant or a Johnson among the list of partners. Or indeed, a formal husband and wife partnership trading as, say, 'Wilson & Wilson'. In both cases, the full names and *private* addresses of all partners are also required on a Form VAT 2. **Item 2** – in the case of a formal or informal partnership with a different trading name, the trading name goes in Item 2. For instance, if Ferdinand Dionysus Smith and his wife Isabella Cleopatra Smith trade as 'Ferdibella Finery', their trading name goes in Item 2. And if they have several shops or businesses, each trading under a different name (not at all uncommon where, for example, a string of newsagents have been bought up over the years and the old names have been kept), then 'Ferdibella Finery and another' (or 'and others') goes in Item 2. The 'others' will be recorded separately in correspondence with the Vatman.

- *Limited company*. **Item 1** – simplicity itself: the name on the certificate of incorporation. **Item 2** – if there are other trading names, then these go in Item 2 in just the same way as for the partnership with a different trading name.
- *Other*. **Item 1** – the name of the club, e.g. 'Moretonhampstead Old Thespians' or whatever the name of the club itself may be. **Item 2** – the trading name – if there is one – although such a situation is unlikely.

Summary

Status	Name in Item 1
Sole proprietor	Full personal name, plus any rank/title.
Partnership:	
(i) Informal, with no partnership name	Full personal names and rank/title of all partners.
(ii) Formal, with partnership name	Name of the partnership.
Limited company	Name of the company.
Other	Name of the club or association.

If your name or trading name is not covered by one of the above, consult your LVO. If you trade under a name different from that in Item 1, it goes in Item 2.

Note: the Vatman will sometimes substitute the trading name in Item 2 for that in Item 1, most commonly with public houses. Don't argue – he's allowed to. However, if you later trade under an additional name, he'll have to undo his handiwork: you were right in the first place.

Item 3 (Address)

This should cause little problem: after all, how many addresses have you got? In the vast majority of cases, it is simply the place where you conduct your business: your home, the office, shop, workshop, farm, builder's yard. There can't be too many choices! To the Vatman, it is known as the 'principal place of business', or PPOB, and is defined as 'the place where day-to-day administration is carried on, orders are issued and received, and payments made and received'. But – there is always a but ... Suppose the shop is too small to accommodate an office and you make up the books at home: which is the PPOB – home or shop? Answer: the shop, where the business is. What about Rock Granite, always on the move, travelling from gig to gig? Or an actor? Surely, his PPOB is where he is currently treading the boards. Or the market trader, travelling round street markets, cattle auctions, country fairs and so on? Or a member of an orchestra, playing all over the country (and the world)? In fact, any business which does not have a fixed abode. So, what address goes in Item 3? The first choice must be the home address – which also means that there must be someone there capable and authorised to handle the VAT affairs of the registered person, and authorised to sign cheques! This may present problems, not least from a taxation point of view. You *must* keep records and make returns – the fact that you were away from home at the time, or didn't have the time to make up the books, will cut no ice with the Vatman: it is not a reasonable excuse. He will argue, quite reasonably, that since you knew you would be away, or short of time, you should have made arrangements for someone to keep up your books. You must therefore apply to the Vatman to have your PPOB at some other address, e.g. your solicitor's, accountant's, agent's, bookkeeper's, etc. Which in turn means that you will have to give them authority to sign returns and cheques on your behalf. This can usually be covered by a simple letter of authority along the lines of:

I authorise so-and-so to deal with all VAT returns and enquiries on my behalf and to sign in my stead.

Signed . . . .

This keeps your VAT records up to date and your returns on time but nothing more. If you want someone to deal with *all* your VAT affairs, you may need a full-blown power of attorney, especially if you will be out of the country more than in, or if you have no legal residence in the country. If the address of your PPOB – and therefore the place where your records will be kept – is not covered by any of the foregoing, discuss it with your LVO and decide on some mutually acceptable address.

If you give, say, your present address, knowing that you will not be there most of the time and there will be no one there to deal with the Vatman, he could come chasing you as a 'missing trader', or 'failing to notify a change in registered particulars', or 'failing to make returns'. All of which could cost you a lot of money in penalties.

The PPOB is also the place where a visiting Vatman would expect to see you, the business and the books. If you choose to send everything to a bookkeeper at the other end of the country, the

Vatman will still want to see everything at the PPOB. You will need a very good excuse for any other arrangement. If the books are kept at a nearby accountant or bookkeeper, the Vatman will usually not object to going there to see the books, provided he can see you and the business at the PPOB.

Item 5 (Business activity)

Only a brief statement is required merely sufficient to identify the general field of trading (e.g. glazing contractor, management consultant, confectioner, tobacconist, newsagent, actor, solicitor). You also need the trade classification number which you will have to dig out of Notice 41, which should have come with the VAT 1. This is the old Board of Trade's trade classification list and sometimes the classifications are a bit broad. Pick the description that most nearly fits your business (don't worry if the closest you can get is something like '8999, other services'). Originally, the Vatman used these classifications to split all registered traders into one of three 'stagger groups' with tax periods running on the calendar quarter, one month later or two months later, so that he could get about one third of the returns in each month instead of the whole 1,250,000 once a quarter! It is also used for computer comparisons of trading profiles for members of a classification.

Item 6 (Computer user)

Either you use a computer for your financial records, or you don't. If you don't, leave the box blank.

Item 7 (Repayments)

If you expect to receive regular repayments of VAT, either because you deal in zero-rated goods and services, or are mainly concerned with exporting, then tick the box. If you want the repayments to go straight to your bank account, fill in either the bank account number or the national giro number. (The bank sorting code is the group of three pairs of numbers in the top right corner of your cheque.)

Items 8 & 9 (Dates)

These items are to be completed only for *compulsory registration*.

However, the Vatman takes no account of a business which has been jogging along for years and only now is over the limit. He has tried to make allowance by asking for the date of your first taxable supply (on the original VAT 1, the question was 'When did your business start?', and one answer was '1794'. The 'trader' concerned was the military band of a very senior regiment!), but, strictly speaking, you cannot make a *taxable* supply until you are registered. What the Vatman means is: 'When did you first make a supply which falls within the zero or standard rate classifications?' Which makes the point: if you have been in business for more than a year, the date you opened for business, and your turnover for the 12 months after that date, are of little relevance.

Therefore, I recommend the following procedure. Work out Item 9 date first (see 'When to register' above). Then work out the date for Item 8, which will be either the beginning of the quarter or year in which you exceeded the registration limit and which has now led to your notification; or the date on which you opened for business, knowing that you will exceed the registration limit in the next 12 months. If the two dates turn out to be the same – don't worry. And you can then give the 'value of taxable supplies from that date' in Item 8, either as an actual figure or as an estimate. If the Vatman wants any clarification of these dates, he'll ask for it, and may also ask for a quarter-by-quarter breakdown of your turnover since you started trading. And if you make the horrible discovery that you are late in notifying, own up, explain why and don't try to conceal it: it will go harder with you if your lateness is discovered on the first visit.

Item 10 (Exemption from registration)

The Vatman is less than helpful here, indicating that the only reason for exemption is that all your outputs are zero rate (see 'Exemption from registration' above). You can be sure that, if you exceed the quarterly limit and don't notify, the Vatman will make life awkward. So get in first, establish your seasonal factor and then go on your way with a clear conscience.

Item 11 (Voluntary registration)

There is no date box here, and you do *not* complete Items 8 and 9 – this is not a compulsory registration. There is another date on the VAT 1, i.e. the date of signing. Lacking any other date, the Vatman may, if he agrees to voluntary registration, take the date of signing as the date of registration. You probably won't want this either. The note to Item 11 instructs you to write a separate letter explaining why you want to be registered below the compulsory limit. Apart from anything else, *include in the letter the date from which you want your registration to run* – either the day on which you will open for business, or, if already in business, some suitable date (for example, the first of a month). As to your reasons for wanting to be registered, it's really up to you. Basically, the reasons should be economic – you can't compete with registered traders if you are not registered; you can't get contracts unless you are registered (the pupil barrister or the rag trade outworker, for instance, who simply can't get a sniff without the advantage of a VAT number); or, with something like a village hall or community project, you simply can't run at all unless you can recover input tax; or the farmer, who won't make real money for several years and, without recovering input tax, also can't get going at all. But you must provide some evidence that you will be making business supplies. Here again the Vatman is less than helpful in asking for the value of supplies in the last 12 months, obviously expecting an applicant for voluntary registration to be already in business. Well, if you haven't been in business, say so in your letter, say how much you expect to turn over and explain your estimate.

Item 12 (Intending trader)

State the annual turnover you expect to make and the date on which you expect to make your first sale. This also applies to a builder who is developing a new housing or industrial estate and, obviously, no one will be moving in for several months. The notes instruct you to write a separate letter explaining why you want to be registered in advance of making supplies. It's no use saying, 'Well, I *intend* to make supplies' – there must be hard evidence, something tangible, like copies of contracts, planning permission, orders to be filled, perhaps tentative offers from prospective occupiers of the new buildings, etc. Or evidence that you are stocking up the shop or the workshop, ready for grand opening day. You should also include in your letter the date from which you want your registration to run. This may be open to adjustment after discussion with the Vatman, but you won't want to be registered from an inconvenient date.

Items 13 & 14 (Transfers & Changes)

The date here will be the same as Items 8 and 9 – you will know the date you are taking over the business! You should also know who you are taking over from! If you don't – *caveat emptor* – you'll deserve all the trouble you get! There should be no problem in discovering the previous trader's VAT number, and if he is coy about revealing it ... what else is he coy about revealing? TOGC (transfer of going concern) involves two different persons – literally, different people. The incoming owner might be tempted to keep the old VAT number – after all, there is provision for it. Take my advice: *don't*! You simply do not know what the 'old' trader has been up to, and the Vatman could land on you for his debts!

So why is Item 14 there? For COLE (change of legal entity). That is, where a sole proprietor, say, takes on a partner, or a partnership changes to a limited company. It is still the same business, run by the same people, but under a slightly different name – or even under the same name: the buying public may not be the least bit interested in the legal entity behind the business. So, instead of going to all the expense of getting new billheads printed, with a new VAT number, they simply carry on as before. It's a bit of a bore filling in a new VAT 1 – yes, all of it! – but at least you can carry on trading without interruption as far as VAT is concerned. And, as mentioned earlier, if you intend to trade as a limited company, but Companies House has not come up with the certificate of incorporation before opening day, you can always trade as a partnership and change status later.

Item 15 (Other VAT registrations)

Either you have other VAT registrations or you haven't. If you have, tick the 'Yes' box and list them on a separate sheet of paper. Don't 'forget' about them – the Vatman has a way of finding out these things, and if he suspects that you are concealing something nefarious, life can become tedious!

Item 16 (Declaration)

The form must be signed *by the person being registered*: sole proprietor, partner, officer of the company, authorised official of the club — it cannot be signed by an agent, manager, representative, or someone 'authorised' to do so.

That should be it, but don't think that once you have signed the form and posted it, you'll hear no more until your first return arrives. Be prepared to answer questions — remember the squash club and the trawler! The Vatman must be satisfied that he is dealing with a genuine trader, especially if repayment of input tax is involved!

Registration refused

Particularly in the cases of voluntary and intending registrations, the Vatman may refuse registration — but this is not the end of the line: you can always appeal to an independent VAT tribunal, either direct, without further reference to the Vatman, or you can ask for your case to be reviewed by the Customs and Excise Department before you proceed to appeal. The Vatman will supply the notice on appeal procedures and all the necessary forms (see Chapter 8).

After registration

Now you are registered — what does it mean? It means that you must start collecting VAT on all your sales. At once. It's no good pretending you didn't know you had to start *now*: as soon as you got your registration number, you were in the club. And once you're in . . . *you're in*! Either you must tack VAT on to your prices, or you must treat them as tax inclusive and, in either case, give the Vatman his cut.

Pre-registration contracts

There is one problem you may not have thought of: suppose you signed a contract before you became registered and quoted a price which excluded VAT; how can you now say, 'Oh — by the way — I'll be adding VAT to the fixed contract price . . .'? As it happens, the Vatman thought of this back in 1972 when the first VAT laws were drafted, and under s.40 of the VAT Act 1983: 'If, after the making of a contract, there is a change in the amount of tax to be charged, there shall be added to or subtracted from the contract price an amount equal to the change. A change shall include a change from or to no tax being charged.' Therefore, you will be quite within the law in adding VAT to the contract price; or, of course, you can decide to absorb the VAT yourself in the interests of good trading relations. And you can claim back all the VAT that has been charged to you for all manner of things . . . Well, not quite. On your first VAT return, you can claim back all the VAT you have paid out *for business purposes* since you were registered, and *for which you hold a valid tax invoice.*

Pre-registration VAT

But what about the VAT you paid out before registration, for the purposes of your business: is that lost and gone forever? Not necessarily. Provided you hold valid tax invoices, you can claim back the VAT on *goods on hand* at the time of registration, and on services necessary to the setting up of your business up to six months before the date of registration. If you have bought and sold goods of any description before the date of your registration, you are assumed to have recovered your VAT in the sale price. This includes not only stock in trade, but capital goods of all kinds, like machinery, tools, counters, tills, commercial vehicles – anything, in fact, provided it is not a prohibited deduction. All this means that you must keep records, because, sooner or later, the Vatman will demand to see them and, if he thinks that your records are inadequate, or incomplete, he has the power to require you to keep better records and to demand from you any tax which he thinks you should have paid but haven't.

Miscellany

Growing

Suppose you have done quite well in one trade and decide to expand into other fields – for example, you set up a catering business to exploit the full potential of your bakery; you buy another business which is already operating as a limited company; you take over another shop with a different partner, and for various reasons, either you have to have a different VAT registration, or you want to keep the businesses separate. It is virtually certain that your different businesses will trade with each other. If you own a string of CTN, for instance, you will probably get better discount if one business buys for all the rest (this is especially true of newspapers and tobacco products). Then, when you distribute your bulk buying around the other businesses, you have to charge them output tax (which they in turn will claim back from the Vatman) and so you will have a chunk of money tied up, going round in a circle, getting nowhere and doing no one any good.

Partnerships

If you operate as a series of partnerships, you are stuck with this money-go-round: each one must have a separate VAT registration and any dealings among them must follow the normal rules, charging output tax and deducting input tax.

Limited companies

However, if you operate as a series of limited companies, you could put them all into a single group registration, provided that one person, one partnership or one limited company controls all the limited companies. Then you can trade among the different companies without any reference to VAT. The representative company is treated as handling all input and output tax, so there is only a single VAT return to complete each quarter. (See Leaflet 700/2.)

Changes in registered details

If, at any time, any of the registered details change (e.g. change of name, status, address, business, gaining or losing a partner – in fact, anything that you put in the first six items of the VAT 1), you must notify the Vatman. There are penalties for not telling him. If you are not sure whether the 'change' is a change for registration purposes, write and tell the Vatman anyway. Better tell him things he doesn't, strictly, want to know than fail to tell him things he *does* want to know.

Cancelling the registration

If your business never gets going, or goes under, you change your mind, want to retire, turnover drops well below the registration limit and looks like never getting back up there, you can apply to have the registration cancelled. Generally it is less of a hassle than getting registered: there is no form, you just need to write and tell the Vatman what's happening. There will be a final return to fill in, perhaps a questionnaire, perhaps a visit by a Vatman – it depends on how you are ending the business, e.g. TOGC, selling up, have a lot of stocks and assets to get rid off, continuing in business below the registration limit, etc. Briefly: TOGC does not involve any charge of VAT; straight selling up, or continuing to trade below the registration limit, requires the declaration of VAT on the value of the goods (stock and capital) remaining at deregistration day. (See Leaflet 700/11.)

2

Dormant business

You may not keep a dormant business on the register in case you find another business or location that takes your fancy: if the business ceases, then so does the registration. In any case, you would still get the returns coming in, and if they don't go back, the Vatman will clobber you with all kinds of penalties. This not to say that, if you are between businesses and are simply relocating or negotiating the purchase of the new business, you must deregister and go through the palaver of registering the new business. What the Vatman will not permit is your hanging on to a registration with no prospect of starting trading again within a reasonable time; i.e. you must be making business supplies if you want to remain registered.

Joint venture

Joint ventures and consortia have legal existence, at least as far as VAT is concerned. If a group of individuals or partnerships, or even limited companies, get together to carry out some common purpose, then, if the joint action amounts to a partnership and the turnover will exceed the minimum registration limit, all registration conditions apply. If a partnership is not formed, then each participant must bear his own input and output tax, if registered.

Purchase and resale of an article may be conducted by one member of the group and either he accounts for all input and output tax and payment of money between the members is not the consideration for a taxable supply; or, one member buys the article, and when collecting contributions from the other members of the syndicate, he is regarded as supplying taxable services, and when the article is sold and the profits are distributed, then those payments are regarded as consideration for a supply of services by each member. Normal tax invoicing procedures apply.

Purchase for use (e.g. farm machinery used by a group of farmers) is normally invoiced to one member. Any charges he makes for maintenance, or for a proportion of the cost, are to be treated as supplies of services and invoiced accordingly. If the machine is sold, shares of the sale price paid to members of the syndicate are again consideration for supplies of services by the members.

Society shows

For example, agricultural shows, steam rallies, craft exhibitions, political garden parties and the like, normally held for a day or two and arranged by an organising committee, may amount to the conducting of a business. Especially where there is an admission charge (which is prima-facie evidence of the existence of a business operation), exhibitors are charged a pitch fee, charges are made for car parking, and, in general, the whole thing is organised to make money, then, if the single event is likely to turn over (not make a profit, but make a gross collection of) more than the registration limit, all conditions of notification and registration apply. Voluntary registration is not permitted in these conditions. If the show is one of a series, run by the same committee, although a single show does not exceed the registration limit, the series of shows may do so, and the show committee must register. Alternatively, if each show is organised by a different *ad hoc* committee and does not reach the registration limit, no notification is required. (On the other hand, why not register a permanent committee, and recover as much VAT as you can?)

Party plan selling

This is an operation of the company supplying the goods and the 'hostess' is regarded as an employee of the company. If a professional hostess works for several companies, she may be regarded as self-employed, and, if her commissions in cash and kind exceed the registration limit, she must notify and register if conditions so dictate.

Unregistered and no longer liable to be registered

It sometimes happens that you conduct a business for a while, perhaps run a society show, and when it is all over, discover that it went over the registration limit. Well, you can either lie low and say 'nuffin', like Brer Rabbit, and hope the Vatman doesn't find out, or obey the law and own up. You will have to go through the full VAT 1 procedure, together with explanations as to why you didn't notify sooner, but you will not be registered. You will, though, be required to pay up the net tax on your operation, plus, perhaps, a penalty for late notification and interest charges! (See Chapter 8.)

2

3 Accounts

Keeping accounts for VAT purposes □ Purchases – basic
records □ Sales – basic records □ The tax invoice □ The
tax point and time of supply □ Tax periods □ The VAT
account and VAT return □ Errors □ Credits □ Cash
accounting □ Annual accounting □ Deposits □ Completing
the VAT 100 □ Computerise or otherwise

Keeping accounts for VAT purposes

You might as well face it: once you are registered for VAT, you
must keep records. No more happy-go-lucky 'cash-in-the-hip-pocket'
or 'what's-left-in-the-till-is-ours'. And don't be like the head of an
agricultural college, with no training in VAT, who blithely informed
me that he taught the students all they needed to know about VAT
in the farm accounts course. After all, nothing's changed, has it?
Fifteen per cent of £100 is still £15 . . . I shudder to think of the
nasty shock some of those young innocents are going to get when
the Vatman starts analysing their accounts!

Everything must be recorded: the Vatman will demand it and
failure to keep records will attract a penalty. Five pounds a day
doesn't sound too much, but after 100 days, you'll notice it! And
it's £10 a day for second offence and £15 for a third, or any
further offence. Take my advice: don't risk it – it gets too
expensive . . . So, what do you need to record to keep the Vatman
quiet? There are plenty of bookkeeping systems on the market,
and most accountants have their own pet system, but, invariably,
none of them includes exactly what *you* want; or what your
accountant wants doesn't allow for what the Vatman wants. You
are faced with a dilemma from the start, in that your accounts
must allow for two different requirements to be handled at the
same time:

1. The VAT figures.
2. The accounting requirements.

What's the difference? Surely, if you write everything down in a cash-book (e.g. sales on the left page and purchases on the right), you can't go far wrong, can you? Don't you believe it!

Trading records

For a start, not all purchases or expenses are involved in the trading account, or, indeed, are subject to VAT at all – like wages, income tax, insurance, licences, interest on loans, etc. Certainly they will have an effect on your profits, but they are not trading expenses. If you have ever examined a set of accounts, you will find them divided into several sections, probably the most important of which is the trading account. This shows trading figures: the goods you bought, the goods you sold and the trading profit. It does not take into account any overheads or other expenses. Elsewhere in the accounts, your accountant will record the office expenses, the purchase and sale of capital goods (like the van you use to go to the Cash and Carry and which is not part of your stock in trade), wages, loans, and all the other drain-holes which allow your profits to soak away. A lot of those non-trading items will carry VAT which you will want to claim back from the Vatman, and having them scattered throughout your trading figures will be of no help to you, your accountant or the Vatman. What follows does not pretend to be a quick course in bookkeeping: all it is doing is offering advice on how to identify and record input and output tax with the least complications because, the clearer your books are to start with, the less work your accountant will have to do, and the less you'll have to pay!

The simplest method is 'cash-book accounting', provided you take certain precautions, i.e. that you separate trading figures, non-trading figures and capital expenditure. You should always consult your accountant as to how, *precisely*, he wants you to keep your books – but even accountants do not always realise what, *precisely*, is required for VAT purposes.

Two cautionary tales

1. The first business had a moderately complex set-up; they sold new and second-hand motorcycles, did repairs, sold spares, accessories, etc. and ran a racing team. The boss's wife was the bookkeeper. They had two tills (second-hand sales went through the workshop till) and declared 1/11 (in the days of 10 per cent VAT) as output tax. But since only the mark-up on used bikes and cars is taxable, they were paying too much VAT. On his

first visit, the Vatman spent a lot of time getting the books right, ensuring that they declared no more than the law required and, equally, claimed no more than was allowed (in respect of the racing team). Eighteen months later, the Vatman went back and found that the accountant had moved in behind him, changed all the records to exclude all reference to VAT, which was why they had not put in a VAT return for 18 months! They engaged a new accountant, who, together with the Vatman, did a bit of horse trading to arrive at a *likely* amount of VAT due to the revenue. Such a deal is out of the question now: that business would now face all manner of assessments, penalties, and probably be served with a notice to keep records.

2. The second business had pretty good books, but when the Vatman started looking into the figures, he could not match input value to input tax. Two of the cash columns were involved: one headed 'vatable' and the other, 'cars'. Since second-hand cars are treated as non-taxable when they are bought (even if from another dealer), the value on which input tax was claimed should all have been in the 'vatable' column. It simply did not match and no one was able to offer an explanation beyond 'That's how we've always done it; that's what the accountant told us to do'. So, because there was not enough value to justify the input tax, the Vatman issued an assessment, which was objected to. The accountants were called in and they explained to the Vatman how both columns included both taxable and non-taxable items. There were licences in the 'vatable' column, while the 'cars' column showed MOTs, purchases from unregistered persons, and taxable items, like accessories, transport charges, commercial vehicles (which carry VAT on whatever the value may be), etc. To make things worse, they were entering cash settlements in the 'vatable' column instead of total value! All this caused the Vatman a lot of unnecessary work, and made things more profitable for the accountant, who should have known better in the first place.

Basic records

What do you actually need for VAT purposes? You will need two basic records: the purchase day book (PDB) and sales day book (SDB). It is quite easy to run both in one physical book (for example, SDB on the left page, PDB on the right; or SDB at the front of the book and PDB at the back). You will need several columns – most cash-books come with a couple of narrow columns first, followed by a wide 'narrative' column, followed by as many cash columns as you could want.

Inputs – cash or credit

Before we go any further, there is something you must decide about how to handle input tax: once you get a tax invoice, you can claim the input tax, whether you've paid your supplier or not. You then have the choice of:

(a) enter the invoices as they arrive and claim the input tax immediately; or
(b) wait until you have paid the bill before you enter it in the PDB.

Many small traders prefer to enter bills as they are paid. It helps them to keep track of their money, and, if a big bill comes in (with a lot of VAT on it), they are often tempted to put it through before it is paid 'Just this once' . . . Let me assure you that that way lies disaster! Having done it 'just this once' in order to get some cash back, it is like the theory of murder: it gets easier each time. But the victim is *you* . . . Before long, you won't know where you are, and when the Vatman runs an eye over your books and finds the mess, he'll start looking for more mistakes and issue assessments which you cannot avoid paying, probably with money you haven't got. Therefore, stick to one system of entering your purchases in the PDB.

Purchases – basic records

Column 1 (the date). This shows the date on which the purchase is entered in the book, and therefore the date on which you claim the input tax (strictly speaking, it is not the date you claim, or get back, the input tax, but is the date which falls in the tax period in which the claim is made). It should present little problem, but don't enter the input tax earlier than the date on the invoice! The Vatman can get very annoyed at this and can make your life unhappy.
Column 2 (a number). Some traders laboriously copy out the number of the supplier's invoice, which is pointless – that number means nothing to the purchaser. However, do number the incoming invoices with your own number and enter it in this column: it will help to find the invoices again, later. Any numbering system will do: a serial number is easier, but there's no reason why you shouldn't, for

instance, use the number of the cheque used to pay the bill, except that you will then have to use a different system for cash payments.

Column 3 (the supplier's name). There is no reason why you shouldn't use a code number, but the name is better since you, your accountant and the Vatman can examine a whole page of payments in a glance, very often checking whether input tax is correct. (Not like the transport contractor who knew all about claiming the VAT fraction and claimed it on road fund licence, MOT, insurance premiums, parking fines, postage, and was very upset when it was all disallowed!)

Column 4 (total payment). Obviously, you will need to know how big the cheque or cash payment has to be and, also, your total outgoings for the week, month, quarter or year.

Column 5 (the tax-exclusive amount). Needed for the VAT return, this is the value of inputs.

Column 5a (the zero-rated figure). This is optional and most times will be the same as column 4, but, if you buy mixed supplies, you may want to be able to identify standard rate from zero rate items quickly.

Column 6 (the VAT). Needed for the VAT return, it also offers a quick check on your bookkeeping: 6 + 5A + 5 should equal 4.

That, believe it or not, is all you need for VAT purposes on the inputs side. After this, you can either add as many cash columns as you like, subdividing your expenditure into all manner of classifications. If you are using a single book for all expenditure, it is here that you will identify the non-trading expenses, e.g. wages, NI, insurance, licences, repairs, etc. – or simply have a single extra column of 'non-vatable' expenses.

Entitlement to input tax

For a start, you must hold a valid tax invoice from a registered person, addressed to you for a supply to you. This may sound obvious, but take the case of 'third party settlement' where someone pays the bill for something supplied to someone else. Probably, the commonest occurrence is a court case: one side wins, one side loses, and the loser pays the winner's costs, including VAT. However, the winner's solicitor did not make a supply to the loser, therefore the loser cannot claim the VAT on the winner's solicitor's bill. Or take the case of two associated businesses, one registered, one not – say, an estate agency and a financial adviser (who is exempt). If the financial adviser decides to buy a computer, the registered estate agency cannot claim the VAT even if they pay for it, because the computer was not supplied to the estate agency. These are clear examples of supplies made to someone else where the person footing the bill may not claim input tax. However, there are other, less obvious circumstances. Input tax may not be claimed on any of the following:

- New cars and estate cars.
- Personal expenditure.
- Goods not for use wholly within the registered business.
- Supplies from an unregistered person, even if the goods or services fall within a taxable classification.
- Expenditure incurred outside the UK (but see Chapter 1).
- Entertainment and hospitality of any kind extended to any customer.
- Any expense not covered by a tax invoice.
- Expenses attributable to exempt outputs (but see 'Partial exemption' in Chapter 5).
- Any goods bought under a second-hand scheme.
- Goods installed in a new house other than normal builders' hardware and fitted kitchen units.

3

Late claims

Suppose you find a bunch of invoices that fell down the back of the filing cabinet a year ago and were never entered: what about them? Just enter them in the book. There is no time limit on claiming input tax, but still be prepared to explain the sudden extra inputs claim when the Vatman comes to call!

Petty cash

There is one more place where input tax can crop up: the petty expenses bought for cash, like a new office coffee pot; some ballpoints; tea, milk and sugar (which are zero rate anyway); typewriter ribbons; a box of screws. A lot of them will carry a few pence VAT. It is entirely up to you whether you want to spend the time scrabbling around among odd bits of paper looking for a few pence VAT, or spend your time making real money, but the same rule applies as for major purchases: you've got to have a tax invoice from the supplier before you can claim the input tax.

Petrol

The one common cash expense that practically everybody has is petrol (or diesel). Ten gallons of the stuff will carry a pound or two VAT, which is well worth having, but you must have an invoice. Preferably a printed till slip rather than a scrawled 'tax invoice': it is not unknown for unscrupulous garage operators to hand out blank invoices by the pad, and if the Vatman catches on to such an operation, he'll make life very unhappy! If you pay for all petrol through the business and make no adjustment for private motoring, the Vatman will require you to declare a 'motoring scale charge' with your output tax to take account of it. (See Notice 700, Appendix C.)

Sales – basic records

The SDB is almost the same as the PDB. The 'supplier' column becomes the 'customer' column and you will need an extra column if you make exempt supplies; column 2 will show your own invoice number, and again, if you want to split up your sales into a number of different headings, you can then add as many extra cash columns a you like. Is that it, then? Not quite. You will have certain capital expenses (e.g. office furniture and machinery, workshop machinery, a plough, printing press, computer system, video security gear, etc.) and running expenses like gas and electricity (standard rate to commercial users from mid-1990), cleaning, repairs, maintenance and replacements. You may also sell off old property, out-of-date machinery, scrap, off-cuts, traded-in office technology items – all of which will be taxable, even if not part of your stock-in-trade. You have a choice here: you can keep these non-trading items entirely separate from your trading figures by putting them in the cash-book along with the wages, NI, insurance, MOT, car tax, interest on loans, etc.; or put them through the PDB and SDB.

If you keep capital expenditure, sales and running expenses separately in the cash-book, you must remember to extract the VAT and put it in the VAT account along with the VAT from the SDB and PDB when you come to make up your VAT return. However, if you keep everything in the PDB and SDB, you are then operating 'cash-book accounting' and you must distinguish between trading and non-trading figures – this is where the extra cash columns will be needed. You should discuss this with your accountant and get everything set up clearly right from the start. This will make the Vatman's job easier, and although you'd rather see him dead on the doorstep than co-operate with him, remember that, the clearer your books are, the less time he'll need to spend with you!

Other records

The nature of your business will determine how much other paperwork you will have. A labour-only sub-contractor, or a typing agency, for instance, will not have much in the way of goods to deal with; but anyone who deals in goods, who manufactures or grows goods, will have to keep every scrap of paper that refers to those goods: orders, delivery notes, packing notes, workshop instructions, cutting orders, mechanics' time sheets and spares used, tachographs, subsistence expenses and mileage/fuel records, import and export documents, etc.

Quite simply, the Vatman can demand every scrap of paper charting the progress of goods through your business, from enquiring about the availability of raw materials, to the finished goods leaving on your lorry – and if you can't account for the goods . . . the Vatman can make you account for the VAT! He can call for cash records, too, and if there is more cash around than can be accounted for by the declared sales, he can call for the VAT on the missing sales. Much the same applies to services: the Vatman will want some proof that services were in fact performed. This is not so easy as tracing goods, but it can be done, like tracing the supply backwards and forwards through the supply chain, checking travelling claims, even working out the mpg against the petrol bought and the miles run by the vehicles. Therefore, if there is a piece of paper relating to a purchase or a sale, *keep it*. For six years! Limited companies must keep it all for seven years, under a different Act of Parliament.

To summarise, then: if you can't account for the goods, or you can't prove entitlement to input tax, or you can't show that you have accounted for all sales, the Vatman can issue an assessment for the tax . . . and make it stick! However, as long as your records reflect *all* your business, you can calculate your true tax liability from those records and he can check your workings, the Vatman cannot insist that you keep your records in any particular way. If he finds them inadequate in any way, he can order you to keep certain basic records, even to naming the records, but he still cannot insist that you use a particular system.

The tax invoice

Tax invoices have been mentioned a number of times . . . What are they? Notice 700, s.VI takes several pages to tell you what tax invoices are, but not really why you must have them. They are, in fact, one of the two basic documents of VAT. Originally in the Finance Act 1972, and now in the VAT Act 1983, it says:

A tax, to be known as value added tax ... (to be collected) ... by the issue of tax invoices and the making of returns.

Without the tax invoice the system simply cannot function. It is the document which identifies the supplier, the customer, the supply, the value of the supply, the rate and amount of VAT, and the time of supply. The law requires that certain information appears on the tax invoice. Notice 700 goes into some detail, but for quick reference, here are the essential details which must appear:

- The supplier's name, address and VAT number.
- The customer's name and address (i.e. the person to whom the supply is made, not necessarily the person who will pay the bill).
- An identifying number.
- The time of supply or tax point.
- A description sufficient to identify the supply.
- For each description:
  1. the quantity of goods or extent of the service.
  2. the charge, in total or per unit, excluding VAT.
  3. the rate of VAT.
- The total charge, excluding VAT.
- Any trade (or quantity) discount offered.
- The total amount of VAT payable.
- The total charge, including VAT.
- Any settlement discount offered.
- Disbursements.

Some of these items need some explanation.

Identifying number

The law does not require a serial number, only an identifying number, unique to that invoice. Most commonly, it is a serial number, either pre-printed on the invoice, or added as the invoice is issued. One trader issued only one invoice a month, so his identifying number was the date, backwards.

Description

A 'description sufficient to identify the supply' must be something more than 'goods' or 'services supplied'. When the Vatman calls for a particular invoice, he must be able to tell at once what was supplied. If code numbers are used (as with Cash and Carry wholesalers), there must be a list of codes freely available, identifying what each code means. Even if the description runs to a couple of pages of single-spaced typing (not uncommon with solicitors), that's what it must be: the supply must be identified.

Trade discount

This must be recorded before VAT is calculated, to arrive at the price on which VAT will be charged. What would happen if it were not inserted in the body of the bill? Imagine a firm sending out hundreds, even thousands, of invoices a day and waiting for the customer to claim discount. They would then have to send hundreds, if not thousands, of credit notes for the overcharged price and VAT, change their output account, rely on the customer changing his input account, and leave him in possession of an invoice entitling him to more input tax than he has paid! That's why trade or quantity discount must be calculated within the body of the invoice before the addition of VAT.

Settlement discount

This is stated after the final price has been arrived at and could be, say, 10 per cent cash or 5 per cent seven days or 2.5 per cent one month, according to the settlement terms. Which means that the customer could pay one of four different prices, i.e. 90 per cent, 95 per cent, 97.5 per cent, 100 per cent. How on earth is VAT to be accounted for? Are there going to be thousands of credit notes flying back and forth? Fortunately, no. Very early on, someone recognised this problem, and in a rare example of common sense, decreed that VAT should be charged on the price resulting from the greatest discount offered, whether the customer took advantage of the offer or not. Thus, on a basic price of £100 with the above range of discounts on offer, VAT would charged on only £90, even if the customer didn't settle for six months and paid full price, i.e. he would pay £100 + £13.50 VAT, *not* £100 + £15 VAT. Although the Vatman loses a bit of revenue, the alternative would be commercial chaos! Usually only a single rate of settlement is offered, but all too often, unscrupulous traders, seeing a 2.5 per cent discount, take the discount off the total price, thus discounting the already discounted VAT, and rely on the fact that the supplier will not pursue such a small shortfall in his bill and will pay up to the Vatman without a fuss.

Disbursements

These are the extra expenses incurred by someone doing a job for you, and specifically incurred for you. It is probably best explained by the following example. A solicitor spends a certain amount of time on your case and bills you for his services – this takes into account all his overheads and general office expenses, paying himself, paying his staff, etc. This part of his bill is known as 'profit costs', i.e. the money from which he will make his profits. Anything which is not part of this charge, and which was spent especially for your case, are the 'disbursements': search fees, telephone calls, letters, postage, travelling, etc.

Some of these disbursements are taxable; some are not. For instance, travelling, postage, telephone calls, letters, barrister, private investigator are all taxable. Now, it says in the Vatman's publications that travel by public transport is zero rate and postage is exempt . . . So, how can they now be taxable? The point here is that there was no contract between the public transport operator, or the Post Office, and you, the client. The contracts were with your solicitor, and these sums were part of his normal and necessary expenses in getting his supply of services to you. If the private eye was not registered, then his fee must be added to the profit costs, along with all the rest, to form part of the total on which VAT will be charged. The items which may be entered after the VAT are expenses which are not part of his normal and necessary expenses, such as statutory charges (e.g. search fees, licence fees, court charges), and which are considered to be the liability of the client.

Then there is the situation where you may order goods or services directly, in your own name, and tell the supplier to collect payment from your agent (a solicitor, in this case). If that supply is taxable, it is up to you to get a tax invoice direct, but the payment on your behalf will appear after the VAT on your agent's bill. Exactly the same situation applies to any other 'agent' – estate agent, literary/theatrical agent, private eye, undertaker, etc.

Now, there is an interesting situation: an undertaker's services are exempt, but that applies only to the essential services of 'the disposal of the remains of the dead', i.e. coffin and shroud, transport of body and mourners, use of Chapel of Rest. But when you order a funeral, the undertaker will probably arrange the church, crematorium, organ, choir, bells, doctor's certificate, flowers, press notice, order of service, catering, transport of the rest of the mourners, and any other special items you may require – all as your agent, on your explicit or implied instructions, so that everything

other than the bare 'funeral package' is a disbursement. (See Notice
700, pp. 68–70.)

Tax point and time of supply

This has been left till last deliberately: there's quite a lot to deal
with, and Notice 700, s.V and Leaflet 700/21 go into the subject
quite extensively, although without saying why it is so important.
So why have a 'tax point' at all? Why not just issue a bill, call it
a 'tax invoice', and leave it at that? Because the tax has to be
accounted for at a specific time. Imagine the chaos if everyone said,
'Well, OK, I'm going to account for the tax – sometime'.
Furthermore, input tax cannot be claimed earlier than the tax point.
Imagine the even further chaos if purchasers were claiming their
input tax before the output tax had been collected! Would any VAT
ever, in fact, be collected at all? So there has to be a specific date
on which the tax is accountable: the *tax point*.

Basic tax point

This is the date on which the goods are actually supplied or made
available, or when the service is actually performed. In fact, very
few people use the basic tax point, mainly because of the difficulty
of tying up the paperwork and the payment. It is still important,
however, because it is the point from which an actual tax point may
be calculated, and, if there is a change of tax liability or tax rate
in the Budget, it can be crucial for deciding which rate of tax applies
to the supply.

Actual tax point

The commonest actual tax point is the date of the invoice, but there
are certain rules about this:

- If the invoice is issued after the basic tax point, it must be issued
  within 14 days of that date.
- If it is your practice to issue all bills at the end of the month,
  then you may apply to your LVO to make your actual tax point
  the date of the invoice. This must be issued within 14 days of
  the end of the month in which the basic tax point occurs.

Unless it has already been issued, thus creating a tax point, a tax invoice must be issued within 30 days of a tax point being created. Failure to do so can attract a penalty, and the Vatman can demand that output tax be accounted for as from the basic tax point.

Tax point 'arising'

This usually happens when a payment is made before an invoice is issued, or even before a supply is made. The receipt of a payment *creates* the tax point, and it's no good saying, 'Well, of course I was going to account for the tax . . .'. If the Vatman finds, for instance, that you have been taking in deposits without giving him his cut, he can demand that cut, plus a penalty, plus interest!

Instalments

What is the tax point for payments by instalment, or through a meter, or by standing order for regular supplies? It depends on the exact conditions of the contract – HP, credit sale, conditional sale or equivalent: the full amount of VAT on the whole supply is due at the date of the covering document and is payable in full with the first instalment. Leasing, hiring, renting are payments for a continuous supply, and a tax point occurs at each payment. A document may be issued listing charges, VAT and tax points up to one year in advance; input tax may not be deducted earlier than each date stated. For metered supplies, the tax point becomes the date on which the meter is emptied and an account is rendered.

Why so much emphasis on the date of the tax point? We haven't talked about 'tax periods' yet, and the point is that the tax must be accounted for in the tax period in which the tax point occurs.

A cautionary tale

The visiting Vatman was inspecting a set of books and comparing the invoices with the entries. He suddenly realised that while he was looking at entries for April, the invoices were dated for the *previous* April! On further investigation, the trader was assessed for a penalty of around £20,000, for withholding tax from the government. Of course, there were a lot more withheld invoices, dated after the April in question, on which the tax had to be paid. An extreme case, maybe, and if you run your SDB a month or two later than the tax period, does it really matter? The Vatman will surely get his tax in the end. Maybe – but the Vatman wants his tax *on time*, not in the end, and he will say, quite reasonably, that if you can keep your SDB up to date a couple of months late, you can keep it up to date on time.

Unknown costs

Suppose, though, you are unable to work out your charge to your customer because your suppliers haven't billed you, and you simply don't know what the costs will be. How can you possibly comply with the Vatman's demands to issue a tax invoice on time, get the tax right and all the rest of it? Well, of course, you can't; so you must notify the Vatman of the situation and get written authority for delayed invoicing, but only in those cases where you don't know what your supplier will charge: it is not a general dispensation to delay all invoicing. But do you really have to go through all this rigmarole for every little sale you make? Fortunately . . . no!

Less detailed tax invoice

Retailers, of course, do not normally have to issue tax invoices at all, but if a tax invoice is requested, one must be issued. Similarly, at the trade and retail counters of spares stockists, builders' merchants, 'bits-and-pieces' dealers of all kinds, where many small sales are made, a retail scheme is not used and all sales are recorded by invoice, a full-blown tax invoice could be a bit of a nuisance (although where a computerised system is in use, there may be no alternative). However, for sales up to £50, a less detailed invoice may be issued, bearing only the supplier's name, address and VAT number, the customer's name, a description of the goods and a total charge, and a statement that VAT is included at the current rate.

Till roll tickets are often printed in just this form (without the customer's name, of course), and if codes are used for the goods, there must be a code list freely available to identify the goods.

Need to issue

Do you, though, have to issue a tax invoice for every sale? Strictly speaking, no – only when you are asked for one. Of course, if you know that your customer is registered, you should not need to be asked, and most trade sales will be on a tax invoice as a matter of course. But if you do not issue tax invoices as a matter of course because, for instance, most of your customers are not registered, then, if asked for one, you must issue one. The customer is saying in effect, 'You're registered; I'm registered; you are obliged to issue me a tax invoice' — as, indeed, you are.

Variations

Pro forma tax invoice

An ugly expression invented during the Second World War by barely literate NCOs aping their officers. If they had run out of a certain form, they had to make a rough substitute to take its place, i.e. a pro forma. The most famous use of pro formas was when Winston Churchill announced the formation of the Home Guard and thousands of men turned up at their local police stations to enroll. Since there were no enrolment forms, surplus 'Lost Property' labels were used.

The word has become part of the language, and a practice has grown up of issuing a pro forma invoice to protect oneself against failure to pay: if no tax invoice has been issued, no one can expect you to account for the VAT . . . Don't you believe it! Although the pro forma invoice is not a tax invoice and no input tax can be claimed against it, that is exactly what happens, and the Vatman is quite within his powers in disallowing input tax claimed on the evidence of a pro forma invoice. Such documents should be boldly labelled 'this is not a tax invoice', but seldom are, and a proper tax invoice should be issued upon receipt of payment, but seldom is. But be warned: with the coming of 'Keith 3', the Vatman can create absolute havoc in the business community, if pro formas are not properly handled, in disallowing all input tax claimed on pro formas and assessing the issuers for output tax not declared on pro formas! (See Chapter 8.)

Authenticated receipt

Most commonly found in the building trade where sub-contractors are paid against measured work. The main contractor will issue a payment document, which the sub-contractor must acknowledge and return. His copy then becomes his sales document and must be treated like any invoice issued by himself.

Self-bill

Somewhat similar to the authenticated receipt, it is issued in circumstances where only the buyer is in a position to determine the value of a supply. It is most commonly met in the payments of royalties for books, patents, trade name, reproduction fees, etc., where only the buyer knows how much he has bought from the supplier. It is also found in the scrap recovery industry where, for instance, it is the refiner who knows how much silver he has recovered from photographic waste, or the weight and value of the old lead pipes, copper hot-water cylinders and the like.

The self-bill will invariably be a dual-purpose document, being your sales invoice to the buyer, and his commission invoice to you. Ideally, it should clearly identify your output tax and your input tax, and you will declare output tax on the full value of your sale, not on the net payment received after deduction of commission. It is also used in such organisations as Marks & Spencer and GUS, who buy goods from thousands of small suppliers (who must be registered to get taken on in the first place) and, rather than disappear beneath a mountain of infinitely variable tax invoices, require the suppliers to agree to self-billing. The Vatman has given his blessing to such operations.

Credit card

A credit card slip is acceptable as a tax invoice and as evidence for deduction of input tax provided it displays all the required details. But be careful of claiming input tax on personal expenses and non-taxable items, liked tips added to restaurant/hotel bills.

Computerised invoices

Do you want to produce an invoice which varies, no matter how little, from the conditions laid down by the Vatman? Then get written authority before you start!

Copies

Some traders use a multi-set document, making up at one swoop the invoice, delivery note, packing note, payment advice, office copy, despatch copy, ledger copy, etc., most of them bearing identical details, and indistinguishable from a tax invoice. So the customer could end up with two, three, four 'tax invoices', and through carelessness, deliberate intent or lack of supervision in the accounts department, claim input tax two, three, four times! You may fairly guess that the Vatman will issue assessments and penalties if he finds this sort of thing.

Only one tax invoice may be issued for one supply, and if the customer is likely to get more than one copy, then either the figures must be blanked out on the copies (what need of pricing on the delivery or packing notes, for instance?) or the copies must be boldly labelled 'this is not a tax invoice'.

Services

Everything said about tax invoices above applies equally to goods or services, except for the basic tax point, and it has to be admitted that it is not always easy to tell when this occurs for services. The Vatman has decided that the basic tax point occurs when everything has been done except for the issuing of the invoice. This can have very practical effects if, for instance, there is a dispute over the cost of the services. If the charge is being disputed, then everything except the issue of the invoice has *not* been done – and if the case is a legal one, the bill can be presented to a special judge known as a 'taxing master', whose job has nothing to do with VAT, PAYE or any other commonly recognised tax, but who examines the pricing of the bill of costs and decides whether it is fair. If he then thinks the case has been overpriced, he can reduce the costs quite substantially.

Changes in liability

From time to time, the law is changed, making formerly zero rate goods and services standard rate (I cannot recall a case of it going the other way), or changing exempt to taxable, and, of course, changing the overall rate of VAT. (Pity the poor garage operator who found his stock-in-trade, petrol, going from zero to 10 per cent, to 8 per cent, to 25 per cent, to 12.5 per cent, to 15 per cent in the space of a couple of years!)

How does this affect the tax point and the rate of VAT which must appear on a tax invoice? As a general rule, the rate of tax to be used is that in force at the time you would normally issue your invoice and create a tax point, but where there has been a very major change in the overall rate of tax, or a change of liability affecting a major class of supply – which invariably means at the Budget – the Chancellor often makes a special rule about when and how the new rate of tax is to be charged. It is worth taking note of, if you don't want irate customers . . . or an irate Vatman.

Tax periods

These have been mentioned from time to time – what exactly are they? Put simply, they are the parts of the year when VAT must be brought to account. When you registered, you chose your trade classification number. This is the old board of trade classifications and was taken over to divide up the trader population into convenient groups; according to the grouping, a 'stagger code' was assigned to each trader. With over a million registrations (more like 1,500,000 now), the Vatman wanted to arrange to get approximately a third of the returns coming in each month, instead of the lot once a quarter. Obviously, whoever devised the system lived in a perfect world: anyone could have told him that people, being ordinary people, were not going to behave perfectly and trot out their VAT returns in perfect time . . . Anyway, the stagger codes were assigned and the system came into operation on 1 April 1973 (an appropriate date?); so the first three-monthly return was due at the end of June – and those in Stagger 1 got their returns for 30 June, 30 September, 31 December and 30 March. Stagger 2 periods were 31 July, 31 October, 31 January and 30 April; while Stagger 3 were 31 August, 30 November, 28 (or 29) February and 31 May. Stagger 0 were on monthly returns. Naturally, many traders wanted their tax year to coincide with their financial year, but the Vatman, still in his dream world, couldn't possibly change stagger codes: it might muck up that beautiful system of getting one-third of the returns each month . . .

The same stagger groups still exist, and the Vatman still tries to put new traders in a group to suit him, still believing that he is going to get that magical one-third per month. In fact, there is a steady stream of returns going into VCU and today there is no problem about changing your Stagger to coincide with your financial year. Just ask the Vatman, either when he comes to visit, or by letter.

Significance

What is the significance of the tax period? Quite simply, every tax invoice issued during your tax period must be accounted for at the end of the period, and the output tax declared, whether you've been paid or not (but see 'Cash accounting' later in this chapter). Equally, you can claim all input tax charged to you in the period, whether you've paid it or not, but you cannot claim input tax earlier than the period in which you receive the invoice (i.e. you can't anticipate a nice fat lump of input tax because you know you are going to get the bill). You have one month after the end of the period in which to send in your return – more of which in the section on the VAT return.

How will you know what the period is? Look on your certificate of registration, and on the right, about half-way down, it will say: 'Returns to be made in respect of the period ending mm/yy and three monthly thereafter'. (Or monthly, as the case may be.) Also, there will be three dates at the top of the return: two will be the beginning and end of the period, the third is the 'get it in by' date. On the right side, also at the top, you will see two boxes, one with your VAT number, the other with the period number (such as 08/91, being a period ending on 31 August 1991).

Change of periods

If your tax period is changed for any reason, the dates for the beginning and end of the period could be anything, and the period length could be anything from one to five months. A first period could be literally any length, depending on how late your notification was. If you have had reason to change your tax periods, take a look at those dates at the top of the return before you start inserting figures. Some traders like to work in 13-week periods rather than calendar months, or periods of, say, 13,13,14 weeks. If your periods come within a day or two of the beginning and end of the Vatman's periods, there's no real problem – just fill in your return with the figures from your periods (but be prepared for a niggling Vatman who will insist on the exact calendar dates). However, if your periods get wildly out of line with the Vatman's, things can become more awkward.

Special tax periods

In the diamond market, for instance, dealers' financial periods are often tied to the 'sights' arranged by De Beers, and since many thousands of pounds can be tied up, they want special arrangements to allow them to recover their input tax as soon as possible. Or take a trader on repayments, with monthly returns, who also wants to work to 13-week periods, which will then very soon get out of line with the Vatman's periods . . . Whatever your reason for getting out of step with the Vatman's tax periods, what can you do about it? Because, believe me, if you render returns with figures for the wrong period, the Vatman can turn quite nasty! However, some common sense was pounded into the Vatman's collective head in the early days of VAT, when he was made to understand the realities and practicalities of the marketplace, and, provided you notify the Vatman of your requirements – and the reasons behind them – you can get special tax periods, but there must be four or 12 in the year, and chances are you will get returns with your period dates already printed on them. You might even get authority to alter the printed dates, but don't do that without clear, written authority, more of which later.

The VAT account and VAT return

The whole point of keeping records – apart from telling yourself how the business is going – is to be able to complete the return of VAT at the end of the tax period. The law says that you should keep a 'VAT account': not a very terrifying item – simply the place where you assemble the figures to go on the return (Form VAT 100, illustrated in Fig. 3.1). Up till now, the Vatman has been pretty easygoing about the form of the VAT account, but the law is likely to be changed, requiring the keeping of an entirely separate VAT account. No more totals at the foot of the page at the end of the period, or a rough assembly of figures on the last page of the period . . .

You will have to set up an entirely *separate account*. The VAT 100 itself has changed, too; boxes 2 and 5 have disappeared and only five figures will be required:

- output tax;
- input tax;
- net tax payable/repayable;
- value of outputs;
- value of inputs.

All corrections, adjustments, earlier under/over declarations, will have to be recorded in the VAT account. This will be most important in the case of previous under declarations (see 'Errors' later in this chapter).

An example

For the present, let us simply look at what figures can, or should, appear in the VAT account. There is a very idealised VAT account in the back of Leaflet 700/21, but it leaves a lot to be desired, though

Value Added Tax Return
For the period
to

HM Customs
and Excise

SPECIMEN

Fold here

Registration number   Period

You could be liable to a financial penalty
if your completed return and all the VAT
payable are not received by the due date.

Due date:

For
official
use

Before you fill in this form please read the notes on the back.   Complete all boxes clearly in ink, writing 'none' where necessary.
Don't put a dash or leave any box blank. If there are no pence write "00" in the pence column. Do not enter more than one amount in any box.

		£	p
VAT due in this period on **sales** and other outputs	1		
VAT reclaimed in this period on **purchases** and other inputs	2		
Net VAT to be paid to Customs or reclaimed by you (**Difference between boxes 1 and 2**)	3		
Value of **outputs** (pounds only) excluding any VAT	4		00
Value of **inputs** (pounds only) excluding any VAT	5		00

Retail schemes. If you have used any of the schemes in the period
covered by this return please enter the appropriate letter(s) in this box.

If you are enclosing a payment please tick (✓) this box.	DECLARATION by the signatory to be completed by or on behalf of the person named above.
	I, ...declare that the
	(Full name of signatory in BLOCK LETTERS)
	information given above is true and complete.
	Signature ....Date ....19...........

VAT 100   CD 1942/N1(8.89)   F 3790(JANUARY 1990)

Fig. 3.1   The VAT 100
(Reproduced with the permission of the Controller of Her Majesty's Stationery Office)

it may be rewritten in time. It will depend on how complex your business is as to how complex your VAT account needs to be. The example illustrated in Fig. 3.2 shows all the figures which could be included, so pick out the bits that apply to your business.

Notes to the VAT account

'A' and 'B' notes

The number of input and output invoices you handle in a quarter will decide how big and how complex your VAT account will need

Sub-totals	Inputs (purchases)				Outputs (sales)			
	Exempt	ZR	SR	VAT	Exempt	ZR	SR	VAT
Notes	B1	B2	B3	B4	B5	B6	B7	B8
A1								
Months Aug Sep Oct								
A2								
Weeks ending Aug 6 Aug 13 Aug 20 etc.								
A3								
Aug								
Page 2 Page 3 Page 4 etc.								
A4								
Aug PDB SDB CB PCB Jrnl Ledgr								
A5								

Fig. 3.2   The VAT account

Inputs (purchases)	Notes	Outputs (sales)	Notes
VAT from Col 4	C1	VAT from Col 8	C2
Bad debt relief	C3	Postal imports & services from abroad	C4
Over-declarations in previous periods	C5	Under-declarations in previous periods	C6

Annual adjustments

Over-declarations		Under-declarations	
Retail scheme*	C7	Retail scheme	C8
Partial exemption†	C9	Partial exemption	C10
Estimated returns	C11	Estimated returns	C12
Imports	C13	Motoring scale charge	C14
Total input tax	C15	Total output tax	C16
Net tax payable to Customs & Excise (16–15)			C17
Net tax repayable to self (15–16)			C18
Total columns 5, 6, 7 (value of outputs)			C19
Total columns 1, 2, 3 (value of inputs)			C20

* For the retail scheme calculation, see Chapter 4.
† For partial exemption calculation, see Chapter 5.

Fig. 3.2 (contd.)

to be, and how many sub-totals you will need to transfer. The 'A' and 'B' notes offer several systems.

A1. Add up the columns in your SDB and PDB at the end of each *month* and transfer the totals to the VAT account.
A2. If there are rather more invoices than can conveniently be added up monthly, then transfer the sub-totals *weekly*.
A3. If there are still more invoices than can be handled conveniently each week, then transfer *pages*.
A4. If you operate something other than simple cash-book/PDB/SDB accounting, then transfer the sub-totals from any book where VAT is collected or paid out, and if there are a great many invoices, then follow notes A1, A2, or A3 as appropriate.
A5. If the number of invoices is so small that you need only a single input or output total in each period, then ignore the first part of this example and post the sub-totals straight to the second part.
B1. Everyone has some exempt and outside-the-scope expenses, and occasional exempt sales which do not all have to be included here

(see Leaflet 700/12, *Filling in Your VAT Return*, the 'Notes to Value of Inputs and Outputs' on the VAT 100, and Chapter 5 of this book). But the Vatman does want you to tell him which items you are going to include or leave out, and gives you the option of operating by 'basis A' or 'basis B' – though, to date, I have not heard of anyone getting rapped on the knuckles for not notifying the Vatman. However, with the coming of 'stage 3' penalties, this could have much more importance than it has at present. So, what are 'basis A' and 'basis B'? For basis B, you *always* leave out: wages; salaries; PAYE and national insurance; transfers of money which are not the consideration for any supply (e.g. gifts, loans, dividends, compensation, insurance settlement, share dealings, VAT repayment, etc.). For Basis A, you also leave out: rent; rates; insurance premiums; interest on loans; MOT, road fund licence and HGV/carriers licences; any other statutory charges or licences; taxable purchases on which you cannot claim input tax (e.g. cars, goods bought under a second-hand scheme, business entertainment, goods not for use solely within the business, etc.); incidental exempt outputs (e.g. interest on deposit or Building Society accounts, sale of own premises, etc.).

B2 & B3. It is useful to separate zero rate and standard rate inputs since it gives a quick check on the amount of input tax being claimed.
B4. The input tax paid out on purchases. Obviously, it can never be greater than 15 per cent of the standard rate column.
B5. If you deal in exempt supplies as part of your normal business, you must record the sales value separately, as it may have some bearing on the amount of input tax you can reclaim. (See Chapter 5.)
B6 & B7. As for inputs, it is useful to record the zero rate and standard rate outputs separately, since it gives a quick check on the amount of output tax being declared.
B8. The output tax charged to customers. Obviously, it can never be greater than 15 per cent of the standard rate column, but could be slightly less, if you give settlement discounts.

Why, you may ask, go to all this trouble? The figures are there in the SDB and PDB, aren't they? So why not just add them up where they are and leave it at that? You may well be able to operate that way (see note A5 above) but, if you have a large number of invoices, adding them up a bit at a time and transferring the sub-totals to the VAT account as you go along saves that slog at the end of the quarter when you'd have to add up the lot. This way, the job is at least half-done when the VAT 100 drops on the mat. Furthermore, if there is an error somewhere, having the sub-totals handy makes for any easy check on where the mistake might be.

Remember, standard rate value and VAT must always match (allowing for settlement discounts).

'C' notes

Whether you have a single total for each column of the period, or have had to assemble several, you now have to decide whether there are any additional items to be included. That's when the 'C' notes come in useful.

C1 & C2. The easiest figures of all to fill in. Obviously, the total input tax and output tax figures from the sub-totals at A and B. **C3.** Bad debt relief (see Leaflet 700/18). If a customer has been declared bankrupt, is in liquidation, or the equivalent, you can recover the VAT element of the unpaid sales invoice once you have obtained a certificate from the receiver, liquidator or a court. It does not apply if the customer simply won't pay – you must then decide whether the sum owing is worth pursuing through the courts, or even to the point of yourself seeking a declaration of bankruptcy against the debtor. Once you have the certificate, you can enter the amount of VAT owing. (But see 'Cash Accounting' below.)
C4. Postal imports. Up to a value of about £1,000 – 1,400, postal imports are assessed for VAT, but it is not usually demanded before the goods are released to you. However, there will be a form attached to the parcel notifying you of how much VAT is due, so you enter it here as VAT due but not yet paid. You also include the same sum as input tax, which may sound a bit of a waste of time, until you consider that, if you are not entitled to reclaim all the input tax charged to you, this is where the unclaimable bit sticks. You should arrange for the overseas supplier to quote your VAT number on the outside of the parcel, or you may find goods held at the Inland Clearance Depot or the Post Office until you hand over hard cash.
C5 & C6. Under- and over-declarations in previous periods are not to be confused with adjustments, which come later. C5 and C6 are for the correction of cock-ups you have made in earlier periods where you failed to declare the correct amount of tax accountable at that time. This will become increasingly important as the 'stage 3' penalties begin to bite. (see 'Errors' and 'Penalties' in Chapter 8.) For now, remember that this is the only place where you can correct earlier mistakes, especially in view of the disappearance of the correction boxes (2 and 5) from the VAT 100. Do not use

adjustments to correct mistakes in retail schemes or partial exemption. In order to avoid confusion between corrections and adjustments, keep them apart.

C7–C12. Under the retail schemes, partial exemption and estimated returns systems, the Vatman knows that your tax declarations are provisional; and they are allowed to be provisional on condition that you make regular adjustments – these are not corrections of errors and will attract no penalties. (See Chapters 4 and 5 to find out how these adjustments work.) Very few traders operate under the 'estimated' scheme, and those that do have had very strict instructions in how to handle their adjustments. If you think you should be allowed to estimate your returns – the only reason for this being that it is impossible to get the true figures in time – then apply to your LVO.

C13. Imports. Time was when you didn't have to pay VAT at the time of import, but accounted for it by entering the VAT due but not paid, along with the output tax, and at the same time entering it as legitimately deductible input tax. (This, in fact, is what still happens with postal imports of low value – see note C4 above.) Now, you must pay the VAT due at the time of entry, but you can still claim the input tax to the extent that the goods are for use solely within your business and you are not partially exempt. This is where you also claim the input tax on postal imports, under the same conditions. (See Notice 702 and Leaflets 702/1-2-3-4-5.)

C14. Motoring scale charge. If you pay for all motoring through the business petrol account, or put all individual petrol bills through the books without making any adjustment for private motoring, then you must add the scale charge to the output tax side. (See Notice 700, Appendix C, and Chapter 8 of this book.)

C15–C18. Now you can tot up the total input and output tax for the period and work out whether you pay the Vatman (C17) or he pays you (C18).

C19 & C20. Finally, you can bring down the totals of columns B5, B6, B7 as the value of outputs, and the totals of columns B1, B2, B3 as the value of inputs.

So, just five figures will be posted to the VAT return:

- C16 – output tax.
- C15 – input tax.
- C17 (or 18) – net tax payable/repayable.
- C19 – value of outputs.
- C20 – value of inputs.

3

It is highly unlikely that any business will have every entry mentioned above, so just pick out those that apply to you and draw up your VAT account accordingly. Keep all the figures as part of your permanent records – don't do it on a piece of scrap paper which you then throw away: a visiting Vatman will require to see the VAT account and trace the figures from the invoices to the books of prime entry (PDB and SDB, for instance) all the way through to the VAT return.

Errors

You may think that I am pleading the Vatman's case, and perhaps I am, but more importantly, I am telling you what the Vatman will expect to see, and if you can produce exactly what he wants, the less time he'll need to spend with you! Unless you make serious errors. This subject will be gone into in more detail in Chapter 8, but do remember that everyone makes mistakes now and then, and provided they are corrected, nobody need get uptight about them.

The only place to make your corrections will be the VAT account. Occasional errors, involving up to £1,000 under-declared VAT discovered in one quarter, can be dealt with by an entry in the VAT account, and the total output tax resulting will be regarded as the true tax for the period. Errors over £1,000 must be notified to the LVO in writing as soon as you discover them. This 'voluntary disclosure' will get you out of paying a penalty on the missing tax, although you will be charged interest because you have had the use of the money. A word of warning, though: if the Vatman phones up for an appointment to inspect the books, and you say, 'Ah! Now, as it happens, I've just found this mistake in my books . . .', it's too late – you'll be lined up for penalty and interest.

But what sort of errors are we talking about? Things like: you turned over two pages and missed out a whole chunk of output or input tax; mislaid a book of sales invoices; entered invoice and delivery note; added in the date; entered goods as value and labour as VAT; deducted input tax on a car; didn't charge output tax on the old van, or some scrap, or because you thought it was zero rate. All these, and more, have been found in traders' books – innocent, if somewhat stupid, mistakes. But we all do them, and, provided you declare them, there will probably be no comeback from the Vatman. What he is really after are the deliberate mistakes and the people who, 'ever so accidentally', overlook a few thousands and get an interest-free loan until the Vatman catches up with them.

Therefore, if you make a mistake, don't look for the nearest bottle of pills nor head for the nearest gas oven . . . don't panic. The Vatman is not going to come and drag you off to the debtors' court or put you into bankruptcy. If you think you have a reasonable explanation for the mistake and should not have to pay penalty and interest, there is always the review procedure and the VAT tribunal.

Credits

Credit notes are a normal part of commercial life and, provided they are issued correctly and not as a method of falsifying the VAT records, they should be put through the books in just the same way as invoices. The sending and receiving of credit notes do not count as errors in previous periods.

There are as many ways of entering credits as there are accounting systems. Some people enter them as they arrive, in the middle of the invoices; others enter them as a block at the end of the week, month or quarter; or if there are a great many, there may be a separate book. But, however you enter them, make sure they are identified as deductions: write them in red, put a circle round them, have a separate column, but *identify* them. The one thing you should not do is to add them to the other side of the books: purchase credits are deducted from the PDB, sales credits are deducted from the SDB.

The sample VAT account in Leaflet 700/21 in fact shows credits, and, indeed, there are businesses which regularly send and receive hundreds or thousands of credits – which is usually easier than going through the rigmarole of 'sale or return', or 'on approval'. So they issue full-blown sales invoices, and when the stuff is returned, it goes, not in the PDB or SDB, but in the 'returns outwards' book (goods received now being returned to sender) and the 'returns inwards' book (goods sent out and now coming back from the customer). In such a situation, separate 'credits' entries in the VAT account would be appropriate, with 'returns inwards' being a deduction on the outputs side, and 'returns outwards' a deduction on the inputs side.

Negative totals

What if the credits turn either the inputs or the outputs into a negative figure? The Vatman's enormous computer cannot handle negative figures on the VAT return, so should such a situation arise, this is the only occasion where you change a negative total on one side of the VAT account to a positive figure on the other side in C5 or 6 (see Fig. 3.2), and if that makes one side 'nil', then it is nil. If the Vatman wants an explanation, he'll ask for one.

Bad debts and credit notes (see Appendix)

Sooner or later, you will be tempted to cancel a bad debt by issuing a credit note. Take my advice: don't do it. The Vatman takes a poor view of such a procedure, and when he finds it, he will issue an assessment for the missing tax, plus penalty, plus interest. He will argue that a supply has taken place, and he wants the VAT on the supply, not on the payment. Unfair? Well, maybe but *caveat vendor* – if you are too trusting and let comparative strangers run up debts which you are then left holding, that's your lookout: the Vatman still wants the tax on the supply.

Is there no way of avoiding this situation? After all, if you haven't been paid, how can the Vatman expect you to pay him? There is a way for some people . . .

Cash accounting

If your turnover is no more than £250,000 a year and you have been registered for at least a year, you can apply to your LVO for permission to operate 'cash accounting', which means simply that you don't account for VAT until you've been paid (and, equally, that you don't claim input tax until you've paid your supplier). In this way, you will be protected against bad debts and rubber cheques; but don't do it unless you get proper notification from the LVO, or you could find the Vatman raking back over all the old, unpaid bills and demanding the output tax. (See Notice 731.)

Annual accounting

This is as good a place as any to look at the other accounting alternative for the smaller business: annual accounting (just one return per year!). For this, you have to forecast your turnover for the year ahead and make nine monthly direct debits to the Vatman. Furthermore, although you have two months in which to make your single return, you have also got to wait to the end of the year to see if you have under or overpaid your VAT, and either wait another two or three months before you get the overpayment back, or find yourself faced with a tax bill you didn't want. Perhaps it is not surprising that not many people have taken up the offer of annual accounting. (See Notice 732.)

Deposits

Are deposits taxable? Outside the scope? Exempt? It depends how you treat them and what, if anything, is done in return for the paying of a deposit. Basically, of course, the receipt of money creates a tax point, so you should include the deposits with the rest of your outputs and declare 3/23 as output tax.

Returnable deposits

If you would normally refund a deposit if the full supply was not taken up, this is your best bet: include the deposit in the outputs and declare the tax. If you have to make a refund, then make a credit entry in the outputs (SDB) and get the VAT back. (Of course, a deposit for a zero rate supply is itself zero rate, and is exempt for an exempt supply.)

Non-returnable deposits

Have you had to do something towards making the main supply? Get in special goods, start a process, but, above all, do something rather than simply note that so-and-so has paid part of the price? In such a case, the deposit is payment for a supply which has been made, and it therefore stays in the outputs. However, if you did not actually have to do something, have you had to set something aside as unavailable to anyone else, like holiday accommodation? If so, say that the customer lets you down and cancels: you will either have to face a total loss on that reservation, or have to spend money getting the place refilled. In this situation, the forfeited deposit is compensation and therefore outside the scope of VAT. Credit the tax to your outputs and pocket the money: it doesn't even have to be declared as outputs. In the case of deposits on hired-out equipment, taken against safe, undamaged return, the deposit is not the consideration for a supply, but an inducement to return the goods in good condition. If the goods are not returned, or are returned damaged, the deposit is compensation.

Christmas Club

This is different again: the money paid in is not consideration for any supply until it is paid out again and spent on goods (or services) in your shop. And if they take the money and don't spend it with you, there's not a lot you can do about it. Since there has been no supply there is no VAT, and even if you charge a small fee for running the Christmas Club, there is still no VAT because it is a financial service which is exempt.

All other payments are consideration for a supply: minimum order charge, small order surcharge, returned goods handling charge, etc. They are in the nature of 'reverse discount' – where a discount reduces the VAT, these increase it.

Completing the VAT 100

All of this should have taken care of just about every variation and combination of figures which go toward the final totals of tax and value to be declared in the VAT return. There should be no problem about transferring the figures from the VAT account to the return, and there are only two more entries to make on the form: to the left of the signature is a box to tick if you are paying by cheque; if you are expecting a repayment, or are paying by credit transfer, simply ignore the box. And just above the signature is a box in which to enter the identifying letter(s) of the retail scheme(s) you are using. This is just one more check for the Vatman to add to his computer coding of your business.

Payment

With cheque payment, obviously, you enclose the cheque with the return. But is there any need to tick the 'cheque' box as well? Surely, the Vatman will see the cheque when he opens the envelope, won't he? Well, yes . . . but accidents do happen. Despite the rigid checks the Vatman makes, a cheque could blow on to the floor or be left stuck in the empty-envelope pile, and when you consider that on a quiet day the Vatpeople at VCU handle £20,000,000 (and on a hectic day, £100,000,000), looking for one cheque for a few hundred pounds – and not knowing whose name to look for – could cause considerable confusion. So, tick the box – you can bet that the first time you don't, it's your cheque that goes astray!

Credit transfer gives you an extra week in which to get your return to VCU: apply to your LVO for credit transfer slips.

Repayment

Just wait patiently! Repayments are sometimes delayed, but if the delay is unreasonably long, the Vatman pays you extra! And *never* put any explanation on the form, or attach a letter, saying why the figures are so different this time, or 'Please repay quickly – I need the cash'. As soon as one of the clerks sees something extra, the form gets tossed out of the computer processing stream and into the much slower manual system, and your plea for early repayment will actually delay matters! If the Vatman wants an explanation, he'll soon ask for one, usually through your LVO.

3

The form

Finally, a couple of points about the form itself – not what goes where on it, but the actual piece of paper. You must use the form issued for your registration, for the right period, not a photocopy of an old form, or one issued to an associated business. There are other numbers and codes on the form which, although they may not mean much to you, mean something to the Vatman, and if he gets the wrong signals, you'll soon find the home-made form landing back on your carpet, with a demand to fill in the right one. This would count as a delayed return, with consequent penalty and interest.

If you can't fill in the right form for the right period for whatever reason, simply ask your LVO for a new one. If you've changed address, you may think that the quickest way to tell the Vatman is to put the new address on the form, but this actually takes longer, because the information has to go back to the LVO to be checked and for a computer amendment to be issued. Whatever the case, always write or telephone to your LVO: they hold your file, they know you. To VCU, you are as anonymous as a grain of sand on the beach and any alteration in your details has to be verified and notified by your local office.

More than one registration

If you have more than one registration, you may be tempted to send in one cheque for the lot, or, if you are due a net repayment, to send no payment at all. Sorry, it won't do. You must remember that you are not dealing with people when sending in your returns, but with a tin idiot computer, which must have the information it wants presented in precisely the way it wants. So, you must treat separate registrations entirely separately, sending a cheque for each one, or a cheque for one even if another will repay you more than the cheque.

Computerise or otherwise

Marvellous things, computers! Take all the worry and drudgery out of bookkeeping – install one, and your troubles are over . . . Don't you believe it! Unfortunately, all too many people do think just that, buy themselves a computer without any investigation, and find they've got something totally unsuitable for their needs. There are many computers on the market, with marvellous blurbs: believe them, and you'll be able to stay in bed most of the time, while the machine does it all for you. Ha ha. You could spend anything from around £100 for a toy up to several million for a mainframe, although the average small business computer would probably cost between £500 and £5,000. And you've still got to buy the program, and programs are legion! They can cost several hundred pounds, on top of the price of the machine (and you'll need a printer, too: the Vatman demands the ability to produce 'hard copy'). Furthermore, what do you need the program to tell you? Do you want 'monthly management accounts'? Or 'aged debtor' and 'aged creditor' lists (which are simply lists of debts (in both directions) that are a month old, or two months, or three, etc.)? Of course, a good accounting program will also tell you your stock levels, stock movement (what's the most profitable line?), staff costs per pound of gross profit, overheads per pound of gross profit, and might even find the leak in the cash flow. So, before you even start looking at catalogues, decide what you want your computer to do for you. Write down, no matter how roughly or briefly, what you want from your accounts. There's no point in buying a program designed for someone the size of Harrods if something simpler will suit your needs. If all you want is a nice, neat, printed SDB and PDB, forget it: it will take you every bit as long – if not longer – to type in all the supplier and customer details as it takes to write them in a book. You could achieve some saving, but not much, by giving each regular supplier and regular customer a code number. But then, what do you do about the odd non-regular?

Where the computer scores over all manual systems ever invented, is in juggling the information once it has been fed into the machine. Depending on the program, it can tell you who owes you what – and what you owe who; a ready-made VAT account; the slackest time of the day or week; who sells most – or least; lines that move quickly, or stick like glue. At the touch of a couple of keys, you can reprice your entire stock; or give selected customers special prices; or block any supplies until the old bills have been paid . . . the possibilities are endless, but will they fit your business? Consult an expert, get the best system for *your* needs. And when you get your machine, be careful! Get some training, and don't be afraid to admit to ignorance of the system. Be prepared for a few disasters, like my newsagent, who spent a fortnight getting all the details of his customers and selling lines into his machine, touched the wrong button and lost the lot! Which was not the fault of the machine, because a computer *cannot* make a mistake . . . It cannot chug along day after day, getting it right, make a mistake, then go back to doing it right. Any more than your ruler, PAYE tables, slide rule or weighing machine.

If a mistake comes out, then some human being put the mistake in. Am I, then, saying that computers cannot go wrong? No. If a computer, or a component (like a floppy disk) is damaged; if there is a current surge or magnetic influence; if some junction somewhere fails; or even if the machine gets too hot, then yes, it can go wrong, in which case nothing comes out right. Usually, the only thing to do then is to throw the whole thing away and buy a new one – they are seldom repairable.

A local authority installed a marvellous new computer to solve all their problems . . . until it started paying the street cleaners about £100,000 a year, failed to pay the executives at all, deducted more income tax than they'd earn in a lifetime, and you wouldn't believe what it did to the rates and stores! This one was curable: it had simply overheated and only required a nice, cool, air-conditioned environment. While its human servants sweltered in a humid heatwave!

If you do decide to install a computer, tell the Vatman at once. Tell him what machine you are getting and what software package you'll be using. If it is a common package, he may not need to come and look at the system; but if you are getting an individually-tailored program, be sure to tell him before you start running. You don't want him to come on his next routine visit in a couple of years' time and tell you you've been doing it all wrong and here's the assessment . . . If he refuses to come, and then tells you you've done it wrong for the past couple of years, you have a good chance of pleading 'misdirection by omission', more of which in Chapter 8.

If I had to put computer advice into as few words as possible, it would be: if all you want is a neat SDB and PDB, take handwriting lessons.

4 The retail schemes

Introduction □ What is a retailer? □ The 12 retail schemes
□ Records □ The schemes in more detail □ Changing or
ending a scheme

Introduction

Obviously, a retailer cannot be expected to cover every sale with
a tax invoice; therefore, the Vatman (with some outside assistance)
devised the 'retail schemes' to make it as easy as possible for
shopkeepers to calculate their tax liability. The schemes have had
two major revisions since VAT started and a few smaller ones. There
will undoubtedly be a few more, but, for the moment, they seem
to have settled down into a pretty standard form. They are all
described in Notice 727 and its associated leaflets. To choose your
scheme, the Vatman expects you to look through all of them before
you decide. Certainly, he cannot direct you to use any particular
scheme, but that has been carried to the point where (officially) he
cannot even advise you on which one would best suit your needs.
However, if you get it wrong, he can order you *not* to use a particular
scheme. The Vatman doesn't even publish a comparison chart of
the schemes to give you a quick, overall comparison. There is a chart
in Leaflet 727/6, *Choosing Your Retail Scheme*, but it tells you almost
nothing.

There are two extra special schemes – one for florists (Leaflet
727/1), the other for pharmacists/retail chemists (Notice 727, Part
IV) – which are thoroughly dealt with by the trade associations,
so what follows is for the guidance of the general run of retail shops.

What is a retailer?

A retailer is someone who, obviously, retails: the corner shop,
Woolworths, Marks & Spencer, Harrods, the butcher, the baker,
grocer, greengrocer, hardware, motor spares, secondhand goods . . .
Just go into any High Street and look around. In the Vatman's terms,
it is anyone with a trade classification in Group 24 ('retail
distribution') or Group 28 ('miscellaneous services'). Anyone not

within those groups cannot use a retail scheme (for example, the jobbing builder working for cash, or the solicitor, accountant, estate agent taking cash).

Basically, anyone who sells for cash, over the counter and without issuing a tax invoice falls into the retailer category. Some till slips do take on the form of less-detailed tax invoices, but the retailer calculates his tax on his cash takings, not the totals of individual invoices. Some retail counters are computerised and issue a tax invoice costing about a pound a time for items costing, literally, a few pence – the only difference between the retail sale and a trade sale being in the price charged. Clearly, these are not retailers in the ordinary sense, and their output tax is extracted from the invoices issued.

Other cash traders

There are plenty of other traders who operate for cash: cleaners, repairers, jobbing gardeners, painters and decorators, all manner of odd-job men, who go to the customers' houses, do their job and collect cash. An increasing phenomenon is the travelling hairdresser and others who take their services to the customer – often, housebound pensioners. These are not retailers, since each sale is invariably separately recorded. This seemed so obvious to a newly-appointed Vatman, back in the early days of VAT, that he wrote a letter to a trader, saying so. His superiors jumped all over him, brow-beating and ordering him to withdraw his instruction. It is now part of the VAT rules! So, a retailer is one who sells for cash (or equivalent) and calculates his tax liability from *total cash takings*.

Keeping accounts

As for 'ordinary' trading, so with retailing: there are many retailers' accounts books and systems on the market. Most of the time, these do a pretty good job of guiding you through the schemes, but they don't tell you *why* you should do this or that. Neither do the Vatman's publications, on the whole: they just say, 'Thou shalt do thus and thus', and leave at that. But be warned: Notice 727 and leaflets for retail schemes *have the force of law*. All other notices and leaflets are merely explanatory, although, if you get it wrong despite what it says in the notices and leaflets, the Vatman will not accept 'I didn't know' or 'I didn't understand' as a reasonable excuse. If you operate a retail scheme, you must do it exactly as Notice 727 and the leaflets describe it.

Variations

There are some modifications to the schemes, but these have been allowed only after extremely close examination. So, if you think you could do it better if you changed it just a little bit, *don't*: you must ask the Vatman first. All of which may seem a bit frightening . . . Sorry about that, but the intention is to make sure you understand the implications behind operating a retail scheme. Get it right, right from the beginning, and the Vatman will need to spend less time with you.

The 12 retail schemes

4

Which of the 12 schemes is the one for you? Some are easier than others; some are denied you because of the nature of your supplies or class of trade. So, let's have a brief comparison of all the 12 schemes (see Fig. 4.1).

Fixed mark-ups

Scheme B2

Food	20%
Children's wear	35%
Books etc.	40%
Newspapers & magazines	35%
All other goods	15%

Scheme C (Numbers are trade classifications)

Band 1   15.5%
   8207 Off-licence
   8214 Confectioners, tobacconists, newsagents
Band 2   20%
   8201 Grocers
   8202 Dairies
   8203 Butchers
   8204 Fishmongers
   8206 Bakers
Band 3   40%
   8205 Greengrocers
   8222 Radio, electrical (not rent or relay)
   8225 Bicycles, perambulators
   8227 Chemists, photographic

Scheme	Notes	Turnover limit	Includes: ZR	Includes: Services	Annual adjustment	
A	2	No	No	Yes	No	In each period: DGT × 3/23 = output tax
B	1, 2, 3	No	Yes	Some	No	In each period: calculate the expected selling price of ZR purchases, then: (DGT – ZR selling price) × 3/23 = output tax
B1	1, 2, 3	No	Yes	Some	Yes	As for B, but: in 1st period include ZR opening stock; 2nd and 3rd periods, ZR purchases only; 4th period, ZR purchases – closing stock. Annually: [(opening stock + purchases) – closing stock] × year's DGT × 3/23 = output tax (compare result with sum of 4 periods' output tax)
B2	1, 2, 4	£500,000	Yes	Some	No	In each period: add up cost of each line of ZR goods bought for resale; add fixed mark-up to get selling price; then: (DGT – ZR selling price) × 3/23 = output tax
C	1, 4	£90,000	Yes	Some	No	In each period: add up cost of goods bought for resale: add a fixed mark-up to get selling price; then: marked-up SR selling price × 3/23 = output tax
D	1	£500,000	Yes	No	Yes	In each period: $\dfrac{\text{TIPP SR goods}}{\text{TIPP all goods}} \times \text{DGT} \times 3/23$ = output tax. Repeat after 4th period with year's figures to calculate the annual output tax
E	1, 3	No	Yes	No	No	In each period: add up cost of SR goods bought for resale; calculate

purchases) − closing stock] × 3/23 = output tax

						Output tax calculation
F	5	No	Yes	Yes	No	In each period: record SR and ZR sales separately; then: SR sales × 3/23 = output tax
G	1	Not under £500,000	Yes	No	No	Similar to D, but operates on running total of four periods: $$\frac{\text{TIPP SR goods } \; Pd1 + Pd2 + Pd3 + Pd4}{\text{TIPP all goods } \; Pd1 + Pd2 + Pd3 + Pd4} \times DGT\ Pd4 \times 3/23 \times 9/8 = \text{output tax}$$
H	1, 2, 3	No	Yes	No	No	$$\frac{\text{Calculated selling price of SR goods}}{\text{Calculated selling price of all goods}} \times DGT \times 3/23 = \text{output tax}$$
J	1, 3	No	Yes	No	Yes	Combination of E1 and H, but runs on an annual cycle. At year's end, use year's figures and year's DGT (compare result with sum of 4 periods' output tax)

Notes

1: cannot be used for supplies of catering.
2: can be used for catering; includes services at standard rate only.
3: can be used if you grow or manufacture your own zero rate goods.
4: requires the use of fixed mark-ups (see below).
5: can be used for services at standard and zero rate, including catering.

Fig. 4.1

4

Band 4	50%
8201–8239 not otherwise listed	
Band	60%
8215 Footwear	
8218 Furriers	
8233 Florists, garden shops	
Band 6	70%
8213 Mail order	
Band 7	75%
8229 Jewellers	
Band 8	50%
Health food and wholefood	

Fig. 4.1 should give you some idea of what schemes can be used in your particular business. Some schemes may not be open to you, like those with 'turnover limits': if your turnover is higher, you simply cannot use those schemes; and you cannot use scheme G if your turnover is *less* than £500,000 a year. In schemes B2 and C, the mark-ups are fixed by the Vatman. Some schemes can hardly be worked without a full-scale computer set-up – notably B1, B2, E1, H and J, which are really designed for big multiple stores who work on line-by-line purchase/mark-up/sales figures. (Although the proprietor of a small village general store/post office, being a computer enthusiast, adopted scheme H, using his own computer program. But most of his purchases were from a very few big suppliers who fixed the selling prices he could use.)

Records

Before we go on to look at the schemes in more detail – what records do you need to keep? There are plenty of retailers' record books on the market, and computer programs, too (including programs specially written for milk roundsmen and newsagents), but perhaps the most important record of all is **Daily Gross Takings** (DGT). This means exactly what it says: the *gross* takings, as recorded each day. So, what's so difficult about that? The money in the till at the end of the day . . . Oh, no! The DGT is the total value of sales made during the day, *not* the money in the till at the end of the day. Have you paid for anything out of the till during the day? Window cleaner, a tip for a delivery man, petty cash for a couple of ballpoints or a bottle of milk . . . And have you taken any trading checks, money-off coupons, credit cards, cheques, money orders, postal orders, cashed any Social Security cheques? Remember what was said earlier about 'consideration'? The money or money's worth taken in exchange for a supply?

Cash payments

If you take cash out of the till during the day *for any reason*, you must make a note of it and add it back to the daily takings total when you cash up. Genuine refunds on returned goods, or refunded deposits on goods not taken after all, can be excluded, of course – but that's all.

There was the manager of a CTN in a prime site in Central London who did everything by cash and ignored the fact that he had paid for his newspapers, the staff tea and milk, the window cleaner, and just about everything else, in cash from the till. Within less than a year of VAT starting, he was assessed for some £3,000 VAT, representing £30,000 of business 'suppressed' from his records, and he couldn't understand why. Well, he learned the hard way. But there is no need for you to learn the hard way: just refer to Chapter 1.

The Vatman's views

Notice 727, s.II has eight pages on DGT, defining it in all its possible situations, including rubber cheques, lost goods and lost cash. Read it once, at least. Remember that the retail notice and leaflets have the force of law and state only too clearly the Vatman's view of things. He will not accept as an excuse 'I didn't know': you are in business, collecting cash, VAT has been going since 1973, and you cannot pretend that you didn't know.

Alternative DGTs

There is no point in repeating here the Vatman's eight pages of rules on DGT, but it is worth mentioning the two alternative methods of recording DGT: **standard** or **optional**.

The **standard method** is, simply, the total consideration received: no credit sales are recorded until they are paid for.

The **optional method** requires that you record the value of goods (and services) supplied, whether you have been paid or not. Which means that you are then faced with the problem of distinguishing between 'cash-on-the-nail' sales, and cash received for earlier supplies on tick.

Do not include any payments for exempt supplies. Do you rent out the flat over the shop, or storage space in the warehouse? Record such takings separately. And add back the value of anything you take for personal consumption. You can either add back the purchase value of the goods when it is time to make up your VAT account; or, if you find it easier, ring up the retail value as you take the stuff.

Till summaries

Most modern tills are very sophisticated machines indeed, with as many separate registers as you want, taxable and non-taxable buttons, product names or codes on the receipt, the date and even the time of day. Where you have such a machine, the Vatman will insist that you keep the daily ring-up, the 'Z reading'. This sometimes varies from the actual cash taken – with the best will in the world, someone will misring a sale at some time – but it should be within nodding distance of the true takings. Somewhere, you should keep a record of the cash extracted from the till at the end of the day and the float put in ready for the next day's trading.

But why this insistence on keeping a record of the cash and keeping the Z reading? Quite simply because the Z reading cannot lie. Depending on the make of the till and the program put into it, it records for certain the serial number of the Z reading – a point not appreciated by a London restaurateur who did two Z readings a day and declared the smaller one.

There may also be the number of individual ring-ups; sub-totals for each register; refunds; no sales; cheque and credit card payments. All of it designed primarily to enable you to get a proper overview of your business and how it is running, what lines sell best – or worst – and what time of day is the busiest. It also tells the Vatman what you've been up to – and if you have an elaborate till and do not keep Z readings, the Vatman can only suppose that you are hiding something. Which he will then go hunting for.

Keeping the Z readings

But where and how to keep all those bits of paper? And for six years! Your personal set-up may decide this: you may want to staple together the Z reading, bank deposit slip, credit card counterfoils, delivery notes, cash payments . . . It's up to you. However, the simplest way to keep all those narrow strips of paper tidy and in date order is to tack them into a notebook, or on the appropriate page of the record book you are using. Or simply bundle them by the week or month in an elastic band and toss them in the drawer, which will only mean the Vatman spending more time with you while he sorts out the Z readings he is interested in!

Shifts

If you operate shifts – say, at a petrol forecourt, a drivers' café, or any establishment where different people run the till at different times of day – most probably you will have them take a Z reading at the end of their shift. In which case, you must keep all the Z readings, of course.

Purchases

Having sorted out your takings, you must now record your purchases. Most schemes require a separate record of goods bought for resale, especially if the output tax depends on a calculation involving the purchases. So, the one thing you must not do is to mix up your goods for resale with expenses and overheads. Most retailers' record books provide separate sections for the purchase of goods and overheads and expenses, and if you follow the book layout, you shouldn't go wrong. But if you make up your own records, be sure to make this separation. This means, I'm afraid, that you have to run two PDBs, and unfortunately, there is no way out of it. You would also be well-advised to set up your goods purchase record with at least four columns:

- Total price
- Standard rate
- Zero rate
- VAT

Very often, 'total price' will be the same as 'zero rate', but where you make mixed purchases (say, at the Cash and Carry), you will have to separate the different rates for the scheme calculations. Individual calculations will be dealt with when we come to look at each scheme in detail.

Input tax

This is the one place where all schemes can be generalised: the only way to get the input tax figure is simply to add it up in the PDB. Record every purchase, record the VAT separately and add up all the separate entries. There's no way round it!

The schemes in more detail

In the following scheme descriptions, these abbreviations will be used: SR (standard rate); ZR (zero rate); PP (purchase price); SP (selling price); TIPP (tax-inclusive purchase price); TISP (tax-inclusive selling price); DGT (daily gross takings); calc (calculated).

All retail scheme calculations must be recorded in the VAT account as part of the permanent records of the business, including purchase price, mark-ups and calculated selling price, and any sales made outside the retail scheme.

Annual adjustments must be carried out on:

- March 31 for Stagger Group 1.
- April 30 for Stagger Group 2.
- May 31 for Stagger Group 3.

Should you be on monthly returns, the adjustment will be carried out annually on March 30 (after 12 periods, of course). 'Own goods' means goods grown or manufactured within the business: e.g. food, children's clothing, circuit boards, or anything else processed as distinct from bought and sold in the same state. Where marked-up purchase prices are used to obtain selling prices, the rate of mark-up itself must be included in the VAT account, for each line or class of goods. 'Class of goods' can be interpreted quite widely. For instance, there is no need to separate food into different 'classes' (e.g. separating canned goods from other groceries), although you may find it convenient to group groceries, greengrocery and bakery separately – the choice is yours. However, 'lines' are to be interpreted much more narrowly: ballpoints are to be distinguished from writing pads; hardbacks from typing paper; domestic plasticware from deodorants and disinfectants and washing powders.

A general word of warning. You will undoubtedly make some purchases from unregistered persons: do *not* include such purchases with zero rate goods simply on the grounds that you paid no VAT on them and can deduct no input tax. Once in your hands, all goods must be grouped according to the tax rate at which you will sell them, and so, where purchase prices are used to calculate or adjust selling prices, goods must be grouped according to their VAT rate, not on whether the supplier was able to charge VAT on them.

Changes in VAT rate or item liabilities

These seldom occur at a convenient time – it is usually in the middle of a tax period. With some schemes – like A or F – you simply start using the new rate, but you will have to work the period in two parts. Other schemes are more complicated, especially where TISP is calculated from the purchase price, and, apart from working the period in two parts, you may need to work the annual adjustment in two parts. (These are other factors to take into consideration when choosing your scheme.) The method of making such changes is summarised in the individual sections below, but you must then refer to Notice 727 Appendix C for the Vatman's view of how to do it. It is hoped that, with the summary in mind, the Vatman's instructions will be more understandable.

Scheme A

Turnover limit	No
ZR goods included	No
Own goods included	Yes – at SR only
Services included	Yes – at SR only
Use for catering	Yes
Opening/closing stock needed	No
Annual adjustment	No
Fixed mark-ups	No

This is the simplest scheme of all. All outputs are standard rate, so the output tax in each period is simply 3/23 of the takings. Show the calculation in the VAT account. If you have a very small amount of ZR goods, you can either ignore them and continue to take 3/23 of the DGT, or record their sale separately, in which case you would be operating scheme F.

Change of VAT rate or liability

Treat the last day at the old rate as the end of a period and start a new period on the first day of the new rate using the new VAT fraction. Add the two results for the two part-periods to get the liability of the whole period (unless the change coincides with the end of a tax period).

Scheme B

Turnover limit	No	
ZR goods included	Yes	– up to 50 per cent of sales
Own goods included	Yes	– at ZR only
Services included	Yes	– at SR only
Use for catering	No	
Opening/closing stock needed	No	
Annual adjustment	No	
Fixed mark-ups	No	

More accurate than some other mixed-goods schemes, but you must keep a separate record of each class of ZR goods bought for resale, and the mark-up applied. Then: calculate the expected selling price of ZR goods bought in the period; treat goods in stock at start of scheme as 'goods bought'. Include only genuinely ZR goods: do not include SR goods bought from unregistered persons. Make allowance for own consumption, cut-price offers, losses, wastage (e.g. spoiled food to be dumped). In each tax period:

$$(\text{DGT} - \text{calc ZR SP}) \times \frac{3}{23} = \text{output tax}$$

The calculated selling price must be reasonable. Obviously, if it is set too high, it will reduce the output tax. The Vatman may check your calculations by using a different scheme (usually D or G), and if he considers that the ZR mark-ups are too high, he will issue an assessment, with penalty and interest.

Change of VAT rate or liability

Treat the last day at the old rate as the end of a period and the first day of the new rate as the start of a new period, using the new VAT fraction. Add the two together to get the output tax for a full tax period (unless the change coincides with the end of a tax period, of course). If the change of rate or liability means that your ZR sales become greater than 50 per cent of total sales, you will have to change your scheme. Notify your LVO and get permission for the change.

If you want to supply own goods at standard rate, or services at zero rate, you must either choose a different scheme or keep a separate record.

Scheme B1

Turnover limit	No
ZR goods included	Yes – no limit
Own goods included	Yes – at ZR only
Services included	Yes – at SR only
Use for catering	No
Opening/closing stock needed	Yes
Annual adjustment	Yes
Fixed mark-ups	No

A little more accurate than scheme B, but requires even more preparation, especially in stock control. You must have an opening stock figure when you start to use the scheme, and a closing stock figure at the end of the tax year (which becomes the opening stock figure for the start of the next year). The scheme runs on an annual cycle and requires an annual adjustment at the end of the fourth period (or 12th period, if on monthly returns). You will need a separate record of each class of ZR goods bought for resale, and the mark-up applied to each class. (NB: 'bought' includes 'grown' and 'made'.) First period: calculate the SP of ZR goods in stock, plus ZR goods bought in the period; then:

$$[\text{DGT} - (\text{calc SP, ZR opening stock} + \text{ZR purchase})] \times \frac{3}{23} = \text{output tax}$$

Second and third periods (2nd – 11th periods for monthly returns):

$$[\text{DGT} - (\text{calc SP, ZR purchase})] \times \frac{3}{23} = \text{output tax}$$

Fourth (or 12th) period:

$$[\text{DGT} - (\text{calc SP, ZR purchase} - \text{ZR closing stock})] \times \frac{3}{23} = \text{output tax}$$

Annual adjustment

After completing final period's calculation, repeat the calculation, using the year's figures:

$$\left[\text{year's DGT} - \begin{pmatrix} \text{calc SP ZR opening stock} \\ + \text{ year's ZR purchases} \\ - \text{ ZR closing stock} \end{pmatrix}\right] \times \frac{3}{23} = \text{output tax}$$

Compare year's output tax with sum of all periods' output tax and enter difference in appropriate box in VAT account for the fourth period.

Change of VAT rate

You must treat the part-years before and after the change as whole years, unless there is only one period or less left at the old rate since the previous adjustment. In this case, ignore the old period or part-period, and do not make any adjustment until the end of the tax year; then treat the part-year since the change as a whole year.

Change of item liability

After the change date, include in the calculation of SP goods which have become ZR and exclude goods which have become SR. If SR services become ZR, you must record them outside the scheme.

If you wish to supply own goods at standard rate, or services at zero rate, you must choose a different scheme or keep a separate record.

Scheme B2

Turnover limit	Yes – £500,000
ZR goods included	Yes – no limit
Own goods included	Yes – at SR only
Services included	Yes – at SR only
Use for catering	No
Opening/closing stock needed	No
Annual adjustment	No
Fixed mark-ups	Yes (see Leaflet 727/8B or list on p. 77)

This scheme applies to quite large blocks of goods and allows no leeway: mark-ups are *fixed*. In each period, add up the cost of ZR goods bought for resale and apply the fixed mark-up to obtain the selling price (make allowance for losses etc.). Then:

$$[DGT - (\text{calc SP ZR goods})] \times \frac{3}{23} = \text{output tax}$$

Change of VAT rate or liability

As for scheme B1.

If you wish to supply own goods or services at zero rate, you must choose a different scheme or keep a separate record.

Scheme C

Turnover limit	Yes – £90,000
ZR goods included	Yes – no limit
Own goods included	No
Services included	No
Use for catering	No
Opening/closing stock needed	No
Annual adjustment	No
Fixed mark-ups	Yes (see Leaflet 727/9 or list on p. 77)

Similar in operation to scheme B2, but fixed mark-ups apply to standard and zero rate goods. Simple to operate, but among the least accurate of the schemes. In each period: add up the cost of each class of goods and apply the fixed mark-ups. Then:

$$\text{calc TISP} \times \frac{3}{23} = \text{output tax}$$

Change of VAT rate or liability

Treat the last day at the old rate as the end of a period and start a new period on the first day of the new rate. Add the two results together to get the output tax for the whole tax period (unless change occurs at the start of a period, of course).

If you wish to supply own goods or services, you must choose a different scheme or keep a separate record.

Scheme D

Turnover limit	Yes – £500,000
ZR goods included	Yes – no limit
Own goods included	No
Services included	No
Use for catering	No

Opening/closing stock needed	No
Annual adjustment	Yes
Fixed mark-ups	No

Probably the most widely-used scheme, because it is ideal for the smaller shop with very mixed stock. There is no need to keep separate records of different classes of goods: just make sure you don't get overheads mixed in with the stock purchase figures. The figures in the quarterly calculation can look a bit frightening at first, but are easily handled by a small pocket calculator. The resulting output tax is less accurate than, say, scheme B, but is as likely to be in your favour as in the Vatman's, depending on your mix of goods. The scheme runs on an annual cycle, with an adjustment after the final period has been calculated. In each period: record the TIPP of SR goods and ZR goods; then:

$$\frac{\text{TIPP SR goods}}{\text{TIPP SR goods + ZR goods}} \times \text{DGT} \times \frac{3}{23} = \text{output tax}$$

After final period's calculation, repeat the calculation using the year's figures:

$$\frac{\text{year's TIPP SR goods}}{\text{year's TIPP all goods}} \times \text{year's DGT} \times \frac{3}{23} = \text{output tax}$$

Compare the result with sum of all periods' output tax and enter any difference in the appropriate adjustment box in the VAT account for the fourth period.

Change of VAT rate or liability

Treat the last day at the old rate as the end of a tax period and tax year, and carry out the adjustment. Start a new period at the new rate. Add together the results for the two part-periods to get the output tax for the whole tax period. If there is only one period or less at the old rate since the previous adjustment, no further adjustment need be carried out until the next regular annual adjustment.

If you supply any services (e.g. small ads on the notice board (SR), video hire (SR)), you must record them separately and not include them in your scheme calculations. Identify them separately in the

VAT account, apply the VAT fraction to the sales value and add the result to the calculated output tax. If you want to supply own goods or services, choose a different scheme or keep a separate record.

Illustrated in Fig. 4.2 is a suggested lay-out of purchase records for scheme D:

Date	Ref. No.	Supplier	Goods for resale			Expense	
			Invoice total, all goods	ZR goods	VAT	Invoice total	VAT
			A	B	C	D	E

TIPP SR goods = A–B   TIPP all goods = A

Fig. 4.2

Calculation then becomes: $\dfrac{A - B}{A} \times DGT \times \dfrac{3}{23} = $ output tax;

$C + E = $ total input tax; $(A - C) + (D - E) = $ value of inputs.

Scheme E

Turnover limit	No
ZR goods included	Yes – no limit
Own goods included	Yes – SR and ZR
Services included	Yes – at ZR only
Use for catering	No
Opening/closing stock needed	Yes
Annual adjustment	No
Fixed mark-ups	No

The operation here is similar to scheme B, but works on standard rate goods. You will need more complicated records because you will have to apply a mark-up to each class of goods bought for resale, and you will have to calculate the selling price of own goods. In the first period, treat goods in stock as 'bought', and add to goods bought during the period. Make allowance for special offers, losses, own consumption and other stock 'shrinkage'. Then, in each period:

$$\text{calc TISP SR goods} \times \frac{3}{23} = \text{output tax}$$

If you supply any SR services, they must be recorded separately from the retail scheme and output tax be calculated in the VAT account.

Change of VAT rate or liability

Treat the last day at the old rate as the end of a period, and start a new period on the first day at the new rate. Add the results of the two part-periods together to get the tax liability for the whole tax period (unless the change coincides with the end of a period, of course).

Scheme E 1

Turnover limit	No
ZR goods included	Yes – no limit
Own goods included	Yes – at ZR only
Services included	Yes – at ZR only
Use for catering	No
Opening/closing stock needed	Yes
Annual adjustment	No
Fixed mark-ups	No

This scheme requires very close control on stock figures *in every period*, and again relies on calculated selling prices. So, once again, you must make allowance for stock 'shrinkage' by way of own consumption, losses, spoiling, special offers, etc. Then, in each tax period, you will need:

- the number of units of each line of goods in the opening stock.
- the number of units of each line of goods bought in the period.
- the number of units of each line of goods in the closing stock.

Then, for each line of goods:

$$\text{unit selling price} \times \left(\begin{array}{l} \text{No. of units opening stock} \\ + \text{No. of units bought} \\ - \text{No. of units closing stock} \end{array} \right) \times \frac{3}{23} = \text{output tax}$$

Record each calculation in the VAT account, including the method of arriving at the unit selling prices (i.e. purchase price plus mark-up, or valuation of own goods), and add up the results for each line to get the total output tax for the period.

If you wish to supply own goods or services at standard rate, you must choose a different scheme or keep a separate record.

Scheme F

Turnover limit	No
ZR goods included	Yes – no limit
Own goods included	Yes
Services included	Yes
Use for catering	Yes
Annual adjustment	No
Fixed mark-ups	No

Like scheme A, this gives the most accurate output tax because you apply the VAT fraction to the total value of SR sales, goods and services. In each tax period, record separately the selling prices of SR and ZR goods and services; then:

$$\text{actual TISP SR goods and services} \times \frac{3}{23} = \text{output tax}$$

There are plenty of tills on the market offering facilities for doing just this, with anything up to a couple of dozen separate registers for recording sales of different lines.

Although at first sight this looks like the perfect answer for a shop selling mixed goods and services, it is the easiest scheme to get wrong. To be able to work this scheme, you must *guarantee* to hit the right key every time. Even if you have, or use, only two registers – one for SR, the other for ZR – you *must* hit the right key every time. Consider: the early morning rush; customers hurrying to work and wanting a packet of cigarettes (SR), a newspaper (ZR), a fashion magazine (ZR), the office milk (ZR) and a bar of chocolate (SR) . . . I'm sure you get the idea. Even if it's not the rush hour, and you run a small general store/minimarket with a couple of check-outs – well, you know the order in which the goods come tumbling past you: the meat next to the pot-scourer, potatoes followed by toilet rolls . . . Some minimarket operators have used scheme F and been most upset when the Vatman has checked their tax liability through a different scheme (usually D), proved that they have probably hit the right key on the till about one time in five, and issued a hefty assessment. (See Chapter 8.)

Yes, it is a very accurate scheme, if you can always hit the right key! Colour-coded price tags and till keys don't help very much, either. The places where it really scores are the supermarkets with bar-code readers; the only problem, then, is whether the computer programmer has fed the right tax codes into the machine!

The usual cautions apply about buying from unregistered persons, and change of rate or liability is simplicity itself: just change to a different key if item liabilities change, and use the new VAT fraction after change day. Show the calculation in the VAT account.

Scheme G

Turnover limit	Yes – more than £500,000
ZR goods included	Yes – no limit
Own goods included	No
Services included	No
Use for catering	No
Opening/closing stock needed	Yes – opening stock
Annual adjustment	No
Fixed mark-ups	No

This scheme is very similar to scheme D – in fact, you graduate to this from scheme D – and the ratio of purchases is applied to the DGT. You will need exactly the same records as for scheme D, *plus* an opening stock figure. The scheme runs continuously, and the figures can mount up and look quite frightening. But don't let mere figures scare you – a pocket calculator can handle things easily. First period:

$$\frac{\text{TIPP SR goods opening stock } + \text{ SR goods bought in the period}}{\text{TIPP all goods opening stock } + \text{ all goods bought in the period}}$$
$$\times \text{ DGT } \times \frac{3}{23} \times \frac{9}{8} = \text{output tax}$$

Second period: add to the top and bottom of the fraction the goods bought in the second period:

$$\frac{(\text{opening stock}) + (\text{SR purch Pd1}) + (\text{SR purch Pd2})}{(\text{opening stock all}) + (\text{all purch Pd1}) + (\text{all purch Pd2})}$$
$$\times \text{ DGT (Pd2) } \times \frac{3}{23} \times \frac{9}{8} = \text{output tax}$$

Third period: add third period's purchases to the fraction:

$$\frac{\text{opening stock} + \text{SR Pd1} + \text{SR Pd2} + \text{SR Pd3}}{\text{opening stock} + \text{all Pd1} + \text{all Pd2} + \text{all Pd3}}$$

$$\times \text{ DGT (Pd3)} \times \frac{3}{23} \times \frac{9}{8} = \text{output tax}$$

Fourth period: drop opening stock and add fourth period's purchases:

$$\frac{\text{TIPP SR goods Pd1} + \text{Pd2} + \text{Pd3} + \text{Pd4}}{\text{TIPP all goods Pd1} + \text{Pd2} + \text{Pd3} + \text{Pd4}}$$

$$\times \text{ DGT (Pd4)} \times \frac{3}{23} \times \frac{9}{8} = \text{output tax}$$

4

Every period thereafter: drop the oldest period's figures and add the newest. Thus, you will always be working on the purchases for four periods (or 12 periods if on monthly returns). Multiplying by $\frac{9}{8}$ uplifts the nominal output tax by an eighth thus bringing it into line with the more accurate schemes.

Even though the figures become a bit cumbersome, this scheme is still quite easy to operate with nothing more than a set of manual records and a pocket calculator (although, at this level of business, the purchase records (PDB) will probably need a nearly full-time clerk to keep them up to date).

Change of VAT rate

Means starting from scratch again!

Change of item liabilities

Treat the last day at the old rate as the end of a period and start a new period the next day. Add together the results for the two part-periods to get the correct tax liability for the full tax period (unless the change coincides with the end of a period, of course).

If you supply any services, you must record them outside the scheme and calculate output tax separately. Show all calculations in the VAT account. If you wish to supply own goods or services, choose a different scheme or keep a separate record.

Scheme H

Turnover limit	No
ZR goods included	Yes – no limit
Own goods included	Yes
Services included	No
Use for catering	No
Opening/closing stock needed	Yes – opening stock
Annual adjustment	No
Fixed mark-ups	No

This is, effectively, a combination of features from several schemes and you will need very detailed records. Really, you need a computerised accounting system. When you start to use the scheme, you will need accurate opening stock figures, line by line or at least class by class of goods, identifying the purchase price of each class/line in stock, the mark-up and the calculated selling price. And, of course, you will need equally as accurate records of all goods bought in each period, plus the selling prices of goods produced within your own business. Then, like scheme G, you work up to a running total of four periods' figures; but the fraction is calculated on TISP, not purchase prices, and there is no one-eighth uplift.

The VAT account must show the calculation for each class/line of goods, identifying the mark-up used, or, if the supplier specifies the selling price, the selling price used, all added together to get the top and bottom lines of the main fraction. First period:

$$\frac{\text{calc TISP SR opening stock} + \text{SR goods bought in period}}{\text{calc TISP all opening stock} + \text{all goods bought in period}}$$
$$\times \text{ DGT } \times \frac{3}{23} = \text{output tax}$$

Second and third periods: add each quarter's marked-up purchases. Fourth and all following periods: drop the oldest period (opening stock) and add the newest:

$$\frac{\text{calc TISP SR goods bought Pd1} + \text{Pd2} + \text{Pd3} + \text{Pd4}}{\text{calc TISP all goods bought Pd1} + \text{Pd2} + \text{Pd3} + \text{Pd4}}$$
$$\times \text{ DGT } \times \frac{3}{23} = \text{output tax}$$

(DGT is takings for the current period only.)

Change of VAT rate

Treat the last day at the old rate as the end of a period and follow the above procedure. You do not have to start again from scratch. If the change occurs in the middle of a tax period, you must carry out the calculation twice, using the new VAT rate for the second calculation, and add the results together to get the output tax for the whole period. If the change coincides with the end of a period, simply carry on as before but use the new VAT fraction from the following period.

Change of item liabilities

This gets more complicated. If the changes do not affect more than 5 per cent of your total annual turnover, simply move the changed items to the new tax category. But, if the changes affect more than 5 per cent of the annual turnover, start again from scratch. Notice 727 offers an alternative method which involves changing the figures for the three previous periods, which definitely calls for computer processing! I recommend using the simpler procedure.

If you supply any services, they must be recorded separately from the scheme figures, and output tax must be calculated separately in the VAT account.

Scheme J

Turnover limit	No
ZR goods included	Yes – no limit
Own goods included	Yes
Services included	No
Use for catering	No
Opening/closing stock needed	Yes
Annual adjustment	Yes
Fixed mark-ups	No

This is another 'combination' scheme and runs on an annual cycle, requiring an annual adjustment. For the first three periods, it is exactly the same as scheme H, building up from opening stock plus the first period's purchases, to opening stock plus three periods' purchases:

$$\frac{\text{calc TISP SR opening stock} + \text{SR purchases Pd1} + \text{Pd2} + \text{Pd3}}{\text{calc TISP all opening stock} + \text{all purchases Pd1} + \text{Pd2} + \text{Pd3}}$$
$$\times \text{DGT} \times 3/23 = \text{output tax}$$

(DGT is for the current period.) In the fourth period, add in the period's purchases, and deduct the closing stock, but use only the fourth period's DGT. Then, do the same calculation again, but using the year's DGT:

$$\frac{\text{calc TISP SR opening stock} + \text{year's SR purchases} - \text{SR closing stock}}{\text{calc TISP all opening stock} + \text{all year's purchases} - \text{all closing stock}}$$
$$\times \text{year's DGT} \times 3/23 = \text{output tax}$$

Compare the result with the sum of the four periods' output tax and enter the difference in the appropriate adjustment box in the VAT account for the fourth period.

Change of VAT rate or item liabilities

Treat the last day at the old rate as the end of a tax year and start from scratch on the first day at the new rate. If the change occurs in the middle of a period, you must carry out two calculations for the period and add the results. You must also work out the annual adjustment in two parts, add the results and compare the total with the sum of the four periods' output tax.

If you supply any services, they must be recorded separately from the scheme figures, with the output tax calculation in the VAT account.

Mixed schemes

There is nothing to prevent you from using several schemes or a retail scheme plus the 'normal' method, i.e. by the issue of tax invoices, provided that you can keep them separate.

The permitted mixes are:

1. Scheme A or F or the normal method, or any combination, in different parts of the business, provided that the different parts are truly separate and records are kept separately, and, of course, that you are eligible to use the schemes (e.g. retail counters for spares etc.).

2 . In addition to 1, any one other scheme for which you are eligible in another part of the business.

3 . In addition to 1, scheme E *and* scheme H in other separate parts of the business.

Separate departments

You can also use the same scheme in each separate department or separate shop, provided that separate accounts are maintained, but not using schemes D, G, H or J.

If you use either of the mixture of schemes described above, it means, of course, that you must keep separate purchase records in each department/shop for all schemes except A and F.

Other considerations

- Change of rate between purchase and sale (e.g. ZR books sold as SR waste paper): record separately.
- Goods on sale or return: record separately.
- Occasional part-exchange: record separately and include full TISP of new goods in DGT.

Regular part-exchange, where the new goods can be obtained only by handing in the old goods (common in the motor trade, for instance) is treated as a repair service and DGT is the cash received, equivalent to a repair charge.

- One-armed bandits: see Leaflet 701/13.
- Gas, electricity and TV stamps: record separately (outside the scope of VAT).
- Phonecards: record separately (commission only: SR)
- Business promotion schemes (green stamps, give-away goods): see Leaflet 700/7 and Notice 727, Appendix B.
- Sale of debts, HP & repossession: see Notice 727, paras 12 – 16.
- Exports: see Notices 703, 704 and 727. See also Chapter 7.

Changing or ending a scheme

Schemes can only be changed at the end of a tax year. When you stop using schemes B1, D, E or J, there are final adjustments to be made (see Notice 727 Part V). Always notify your LVO. If you want to change at any other time, you must explain why to your LVO and obtain written permission before making the change.

Own goods and services

Where these cannot be accommodated within the chosen scheme, there is no need to go looking for a different scheme with probably more complicated calculations – provided you are prepared to keep a separate record of such sales and combine the calculated output tax with the main scheme, in the VAT account.

5 Partial exemption

Partial exemption □ Self-supplies □ Outside the scope of VAT
□ Variable liability

Partial exemption

What is it? What does it mean? It means that you are dealing partly
in taxable supplies and partly in exempt supplies. For quick
reference, these are the exempt headings (see Leaflet 701/39):

- Land
- Insurance
- Postal services
- Betting, gaming and lotteries
- Finance
- Education
- Health and welfare
- Burial and cremation
- Trade unions and professional bodies
- Sports competitions
- Works of art etc.

The rules have had two very major changes since VAT began,
plus a few small ones, and partial exemption is probably the most
hated subject in the whole VAT calendar – hated not least by the
Vatman himself! But how does a small business get involved with
any of these subjects? After all, postal services are the monopoly
of the Post Office; education happens in schools and colleges; finance
– well, that's what banks and finance companies get up to; health
is doctors and hospitals; and trade unions are hardly likely to crop
up in a High Street shop! However, almost anybody can get involved
with land: letting the flat over the shop, or a cottage on the farm,
or even running a whole block of flats as well as, say, a builder's
business or a string of CTNs. (Land, incidentally, does not include
any sort of hotel or holiday accommodation, which is always taxable
– see Leaflet 701/39, *Exempt Schedule*, Group 1.) Then there is
agricultural land, forestry, building development sites . . . The
'normal' situation with land will be dealt with along with all the

other exempt items, but the situation can vary, as will be explained in 'Variable liability' later in the chapter.

And then outside the big cities, it is the local builder or car-hire operator who is the undertaker . . . Pity the poor chauffeur-hire operator who was always being hired by the undertakers; he realised that they were making far more money than he was, so he decided to become an undertaker. It was three years before his accountant noticed that he wasn't applying the partial exemption rules, and another 18 months before the Vatman finally got everything sorted out! (Why hadn't the Vatman himself found out about it? For the simple reason that, as a mere chauffeur-hire operator with a not very high turnover, he wasn't due for a visit.) And what about solicitors, accountants, estate agents, motor and radio/electronics dealers who arrange insurance, loans, mortgages, HP . . .? Do you own any antiques? Perhaps you would like to sell a few to raise a bit of money for the business. Or are you heavily into sports programmes as well as running a taxable business? Are you involved in YTS or restart training? Do you run a nursing home? Not merely a retirement home, but a place where medical care is provided. If that care should include alternative medicine, it is not included in the exemption, even though acupuncture, osteopathy, etc. may succeed where orthodox medicine fails. Thus, a doctor in private practice (as, for instance, at a nursing home), who is also qualified in an alternative technique, is exempt for orthodox medicine, but taxable for alternative treatment (subject to the registration limit).

Who, then, will be partially exempt? Almost anybody! Partial exemption applies not only to those with taxable supplies and some exempt outputs, but also to those who normally engage in exempt outputs and have some taxable supplies. So, just because you are running a small trade union or professional association, don't think that you don't have to register in respect of trading operations, such as selling club ties, blazer badges, engraved tankards and the like, or running holidays, or cut-price trading concessions. A charity, too, which has trading operations, must register in respect of its taxable supplies, and may find itself partially exempt and partially outside the scope of VAT — more of which later.

The principally-taxable trader may have to forgo some of his input tax, while the principally-exempt organisation may be able to recover input tax it thought was lost! And almost anybody could fall foul of the basic rule of partial exemption if they are not prepared for it.

Basic rule of partial exemption

You may not recover input tax which relates to exempt outputs, but, if the input tax which relates to exempt outputs is sufficiently small, you may fall within the *de minimis* rules and be treated as fully taxable.

So, just where do you stand? Can you claim all your input tax or not? Do you have to keep a record of every chance item of exempt supplies that may crop up? Fortunately, no.

Incidental exempt outputs

The following may be ignored for the purposes of deciding whether you are partially exempt, provided they are *incidental* to the main business (see the proviso below):

- Taking a deposit of money.
- Arranging insurance (e.g. on a house, a car, a bike, a tv, etc.).
- Arranging HP.
- Arranging a mortgage.
- Letting property (the flat over the shop; excess warehouse space, a block of flats, etc.).
- Assignment of debts.

However, in the case of lettings, there is a limit of £1,000 input tax per year relating to all lettings you may have (excluding holiday lets which are taxable) − and that is a total of nearly £8,000 a year spent on the property alone. Merely selling goods on HP does not make you partially exempt − it is making arrangements for HP, i.e. putting up the finance, which makes you partially exempt. For the rest, if you engage in such activities on such a scale or with such regularity as to constitute a separate business in its own right, then it is no longer incidental and cannot be excluded from partial exemption considerations.

If you engage in any other exempt activities in the finance and insurance fields, e.g. investments, share dealing, mortgages, money lending, etc. (see Notice 706, para. 10), then you may not ignore any of the exempt items listed above. However, if you have other exempt outputs in addition to those given above, not in the finance or insurance fields, you cannot exclude property lettings, although you can still ignore the rest.

Confused? Well, I did warn you that everybody hates partial exemption! Read it through again, slowly, and make a note of exactly what exempt outputs you have, and I think it will come clear.

Non-incidental exempt outputs

For ease of reference, the Vatman has invented another term a bit like 'input tax' to identify particular items of tax: 'input tax relating to exempt outputs' becomes 'exempt input tax'. So who is engaged in 'deliberate' exempt outputs? Obviously, anyone making exempt supplies: please refer back to the list at the beginning of this chapter. However, before you can start working out your partial exemption, there is another condition to be taken into account.

Other non-deductible input tax

Now, refer to the 'basic rule' again: you cannot claim deduction of exempt input tax. But, before you can start working out whether you are fully taxable or not, there are some items of input tax which are non-deductible for reasons other than partial exemption and which must be excluded from the accounts before you start looking at exempt input tax. You may not deduct input tax on:

- The purchase of cars.
- Goods not for use wholly within the business (i.e. partly for private use or shared with someone else).
- Built-in furniture other than normal builders' fixtures.
- Business entertainment and hospitality of all kinds.
- Supplies to other persons (even if you foot the bill).
- Personal expenditure.
- Non-business expenditure (see outside the scope).
- Goods bought under a second-hand scheme.
- Supplies from unregistered persons.

Capital goods

From April 1990, there will be a change in the treatment of capital goods which are used for both taxable and exempt supplies, starting with computers, and land and buildings. Basically, the cost of the capital goods will be included in the partial exemption calculation for the year in which they were bought. Then, over the next five years for computers, or ten years for land and buildings, if the ratio of taxable to exempt outputs changes significantly, you will have to amend the amount of input tax claimed on the capital goods. (See Leaflet 706.)

Non-deductible (exempt) input tax

How is this to be picked out? There are two methods: the standard and the special.

Standard method

This requires you to identify to the fullest extent possible, specific items of input tax which can be attributed directly to taxable or exempt outputs. This means, in effect, running three PDBs: one for inputs attributable to exempt outputs; one for inputs attributable to taxable outputs, and one for inputs attributable to neither. Then, in each tax period, add up the input tax attributable to taxable outputs (including input tax on goods bought and sold in the same state), and a proportion of the non-attributable input tax. The easiest way to do this is to apply the ratio of taxable outputs to all outputs:

$$\text{Non-attributable input tax} \times \frac{\text{taxable outputs}}{\text{total outputs}} =$$
$$\text{deductible portion of non-attributable input tax}$$

Or you could use the ratio of directly attributable (deductible) input tax to total input tax, or any other method which gives a fair result – discuss it with your LVO before you start!

Special method

This can be almost anything! Where it is virtually impossible to make direct attribution – say, because you use common stocks for both taxable and exempt outputs (like the undertaker who was also a coffin wholesaler and so could not attribute coffin purchases directly to either part of the business) – then you must devise some method which gives a fair result. Ratio of taxable outputs to total outputs applied to total input tax; ratio of numbers of taxable transactions to total transactions; ratio of staff-time spent on each side of the business, etc. Again, discuss the proposed method with your LVO before you start to use it. And if the Vatman considers that it will not give a fair result, you'll have to think of something else.

De minimis

Having slogged through all this, you may then discover that you are fully taxable and can deduct all your input tax (apart from input tax which is non-deductible for reasons other than partial exemption), because the exempt input tax is less than one of the following *de minimis* levels:

- Less than £100 per month.
- Less than £250 per month and less than 50 per cent of all input tax.
- Less than £500 per month and less than 25 per cent of all input tax.

The figures must be looked at on an annual basis, and the figures of £100, £250 and £500 are *monthly averages* (i.e. £1,200, £3,000 and £6,000 a year input tax). If your exempt input tax does not fall within one of these bands, e.g. if it came to £200 a month but made up 60 per cent of all input tax, then the whole sum would count towards the partial exemption calculation, not just the excess over the *de minimis* figure.

Why go through all the palaver of attribution and ratios before looking at the *de minimis* rules? Isn't it going to be obvious whether you fall within the *de minimis* rules? Well, it *might* be. And if it isn't, you must apply the apportionment rules *first*, to see just what total and percentage of your input tax is non-deductible. Only then can you see whether it does indeed fall within *de minimis*.

Input tax deductible in the tax period

You must go through the apportionment procedure in each tax period if you cannot guarantee to be below *de minimis* every time. If the total of non-deductible input tax, and/or the percentage, is greater than the *de minimis* levels quoted above, then, for that period, you must forgo that portion of your input tax. Equally, if exempt input tax is below *de minimis* in the period, then you do not have to restrict your input tax in that period. Even if you think that exempt input tax will be below the *de minimis* level in this period, you must still go through the calculation, just to prove it.

Annual adjustment

At the end of the tax year (March 31 for Stagger Group 0 and 1, April 30 for Stagger Group 2, May 31 for Stagger Group 3), you must calculate the deductible/non-deductible input tax for the year as a whole and compare the result with the four periods' input tax – very much as you would for a retail scheme – and enter the difference in the appropriate adjustment box in the VAT account, showing all calculations. It may be that, for the year as a whole, you fall within one of the *de minimis* limits and you claim back all the input tax you had to forgo earlier. So, is there any way of avoiding chasing exempt input tax around your books, only to claim it all back, later? If, for instance, all your exempt input tax falls in one or two periods, regular as clockwork, and, on an annual basis, you are always below the *de minimis* levels, write to your LVO explaining the point and ask to be relieved of the quarterly exempt input tax 'juggling'. You may still be required to perform the annual calculation, just to prove that you were right.

If there is any other situation whereby, on an annual basis, you can show that you will always be below the *de minimis* limits, discuss it with your LVO. Don't simply ignore it: you can be sure that, on the next Vatman's visit, you will be outside the *de minimis* limits and get landed with an assessment! However, if you cannot guarantee that you will be within the *de minimis* levels every year, then you must go through the exempt input tax performance every period. It's a bit like minesweeping: you have to sweep the Swept Channel just to prove that it is clear. In just the same way, you have to go through the partial exemption performance to prove that you are fully taxable.

Group registrations

If one member of a group registration is partially exempt, even wholly exempt, then the group is partially exempt, and the representative member will do all the calculation and declaration. And it might just turn out that, where the individual company was partially exempt and unable to reclaim all its input tax (or even unable to register!), the Group will be fully taxable under the *de minimis* rules. Or, if the exempt member makes supplies only to other group members, the group as a whole will not be making exempt supplies anyway, and so need not even consider partial exemption! But don't assume it! Discuss it with your LVO, although there should be no refusal to register such a group.

Self-supplies

Self-supply of stationery

Plenty of businesses produce their own stationery – that is, *printed matter*, not just the ordinary day-to-day typing and photocopying:

forms, billheads, letterheads, brochures, leaflets, instructions and the like. Stuff which would normally be bought from a professional printer, but, because of the scale of the operation, the business can produce cheaper, cutting out the middleman. With a fully-taxable business, this makes no difference to the revenue, because whatever VAT the printer might charge, the fully-taxable business would deduct as input tax. (See Leaflet 706/1.) However, where that same printer would supply printed matter to an exempt or partially exempt business, the VAT (or some of it) would stick. Therefore, when such a business does its own printing more cheaply in-house, the revenue loses out on the *value added*.

The Vatman has made special rules where the exempt or partially exempt business produces its own printed matter.

Exempt business

If the value of the in-house printing – consisting of full production costs of materials and services, *and* a proportion of overheads – exceeds the minimum registration limit, then that business must register in respect of its self-supplies of stationery and treat the registered business as a separate business, selling stationery to the exempt business. If the bulk of the stationery so produced is zero rate (see Leaflet 701/10), the registered business may well end up as a regular repayment trader – but the Vatman cannot then turn round and cancel the registration! More usually, the supply will be mainly standard rate and the tax will stick, to the benefit of the revenue.

Partially exempt business

Again, if the value of your in-house printing exceeds the minimum registration limit and you are required to apportion your input tax on account of exempt outputs, then: if the bulk of your printing is zero rate, *or*, if standard rate, it is attributable to the taxable (standard and zero rate) side of the business, so that the net tax arising from the printing operations is negligible. You should apply to your LVO for written confirmation that you need not include the printing in your input tax calculations.

However, if an appreciable portion of your printing is standard rate (see Leaflet 701/10) *and* is attributable to the exempt side of the business, you will have to adjust your VAT. You may deduct all the VAT on the goods and services bought in to produce the printed matter; but then you must treat the output tax on the printed matter (declared on the outputs side of the VAT account) as input tax, and attribute it to the taxable and exempt parts of the business. Which is where some of the tax sticks. You must, obviously, keep records of your printing operations and apportion the input tax in the same way that you apportion other input tax. But, as ever, be sure you have the written approval of your local VAT office.

Outside the scope of VAT

This has been mentioned before, but now is the time to look at it a little more closely. And the first thing to be mentioned is that there are two sorts of 'outside the scope':

1. Outside-the-scope business.
2. Outside-the-scope non-business.

What is the difference? In the same way that some input tax is non-deductible because the law says so, and some is non-deductible because of the purpose to which it is put, so some supplies are outside the scope of VAT either because they are not *supplies in the course of business*, or because of where or how they are supplied.

Take the case of an importer who finds a buyer for his goods before they reach Britain, and sells them while they are still on the high seas – or even at high altitude. That deal is outside the scope of VAT because it effectively took place outside Britain – and outside of the jurisdiction of VAT law. However, it was *business*, and therefore there is no restriction on the deduction of input tax relating to the business.

On the other hand, take the case of a registered trader who has outside the scope operations within the country; most usually, this would be a charity, registered in respect of its taxable trading activities, but could be any business which finances non-business operations through its business accounts. Obviously, the charitable activities are *not* business, but the bookkeeping and financial structure may be such that purchases for each side of the organisation cannot be easily separated. Or, the operations of the business may be supported or funded by unconditional grant (that is, the person making the grant receives nothing in return for his money, although, if his name is so much as mentioned as making the grant, he receives the service of publicity or advertising and the grant is no longer unconditional), so that a portion of the trade is outside the scope.

So, input tax relating to outside the scope non-business is not deductible *and* there is no *de minimis* rule as there is for partial exemption. It will then be necessary to conduct a partial-exemption-type exercise to determine the amount of non-deductible input tax. Remember, any activity carried on by a registered person which is not business is then outside the scope of VAT and no related input tax may be deducted. But a garage conducting MOT tests (which are outside the scope of VAT, being a statutory charge) does not have to forgo related input tax because it is effectively supplying taxable agent's services to the Ministry of Transport.

Foreign trading

What about the trader whose business takes him abroad? Surely he is conducting business outside the UK (and EC, often) which is therefore outside the scope of VAT; if he also conducts a registrable amount of business inside the UK, how does he come off for input tax? Don't fret! He is in the same position as the importer who sells his cargo on the high seas: he is conducting *business*, and any input tax he incurs in the UK which relates to his business is deductible. And, of course, come 1992, input tax incurred in other member states will be deductible through his UK registration.

Variable liability

This was hinted at when discussing exempt supplies of rights over land (lettings) in 'Partial exemption' above. Now is the time to examine it more closely, and it is the only liability question to be dealt with in these pages. Variable liability affects five classes of supply:

1. Safety boots and helmets.
2. Fuel and power.
3. Water and sewerage.
4. Land and property.
5. Building.

It all comes about from our losing a case at the European Court, which means that, in general, we can no longer make exempt or zero rate supplies to persons in business – registered or not.

Safety boots and helmets

This is a funny one! If an employer buys protective boots and helmets (to British Standards) for the use of his employees, the supply will be standard rate (but if the employee goes and buys his own, it is zero rate!). Motorcycle crash helmets and horsemen's hard hats remain zero-rated, and so do wholesale supplies. It is only the employer buying for his employees who must pay the tax. (See Leaflet 701/23/89, *Protective Boots and Helmets*.)

Fuel and power

From 1 July 1990, supplies of fuel and power (that is, basically, gas and electricity) – which are all currently zero rate – will become standard rate for commercial users. Where you have separate gas and electricity meters for domestic and commercial use, there should be little problem, but where one meter supplies both . . . well, you'd better get either a check-meter installed for one or the other, or entirely separate-metered supplies. Bottled gas, solid fuel and tanker supplies also present little problem; zero-rated supplies (whether delivered for domestic/charity use or not) will be:

- 1 tonne of coal or coke, or any amount of wood or peat.
- 2,000 litres (440 gallons) of LPG (liquefied petroleum gas), or a 50-kilogram cylinder.
- 2,300 litres (506 gallons) of domestic heating oil, kerosene (paraffin) or 'red diesel'.
- piped gas – 5 therms per day.
- electricity – 33 kilowatt-hours per day.

And in addition, if 60 per cent or more of a mixed (domestic and business) supply qualifies for zero-rating, the whole supply may be zero-rated. At less than 60 per cent 'qualifying use' (i.e. zero-rated), tax must be charged on the non-qualifying portion. (See VAT Information Sheet 2/89 and Leaflet 701/19/87.)

Larger quantities

Anyone wanting a larger delivery for domestic use – say, a big block of flats or a residential caravan site – will have to give the supplier a certificate stating that he is entitled to zero rate supplies. Although current thinking is that the Vatman will go after the consumer for the tax if he gives a false certificate, suppliers had better be very careful about accepting a certificate of entitlement without sufficient checking that the customer really is entitled to zero rating.

Water and sewerage

Virtually the same conditions apply here, although, since there is no general metering of the supplies as yet, it must be supposed that the regional water boards will base taxable (i.e. standard rate) charges on some arbitrary assessment. (See the new Leaflet 701/16/89 *Sewerage Services and Water*.)

Land and building

This, unfortunately, is much more complicated, and the Vatman has produced Notices 742 A and B on the subject. You will also need Leaflets 708/1,2,3,4; plus Notice 706 *Partial Exemption* (it can still apply).

If you propose to build your own buildings on your own land, i.e. make a self-supply of building services, refer to Leaflet 708/2/89, para. 4. This self-supply will operate much like the self-supply of stationery, but there is a lower limit of a cost of £100,000 or an increase in floor space of 10 per cent. What follows, then, is only a summary of the main points: for the full liability details, you must consult Notices 742 A and B.

New construction

Until the 1989 Budget, any new construction (or demolition) was zero-rated and any work to any building for any purpose was taxable at standard rate. Now, new domestic accommodation and charity non-business buildings may be constructed at zero rate, but everything else is taxable at standard rate, including demolition. There is just one exception: where a listed building is to be altered, under a 'listed building consent', if it is, or will be when altered, a domestic dwelling or other qualifying building, the alteration may be zero-rated. Any consequential repair, maintenance or decoration (rewiring, replumbing, damp-proofing, etc.) is standard rate.

This is fine for the registered taxable builder, supplying labour and materials. However, the way in which a new building is supplied may affect its tax status, and it could be standard rate, zero rate or exempt.

NOTE: Apart from domestic accommodation, anyone claiming entitlement to zero-rating must give the builder or other person constructing a building a certificate in accordance with Leaflet 708/4/89.

Domestic or other qualifying construction
Grant of major interest (i.e. sale or lease for a term certain exceeding 21 years):
sale = zero rate.
lease = first payment zero rate, all subsequent payments exempt.
Grant of minor interest (i.e. rent or lease for a period less than 21 years):
rent or lease = exempt.

All other buildings
Grant of major interest:
sale = taxable at standard rate.
lease = taxable at standard rate.
Grant of minor interest:
rent or lease = exempt (unless the option to tax is chosen).

5

> NOTE: A lease for less than 21 years, plus a 'reversionary lease' executed at the same time – which together total more than 21 years – constitute a grant of major interest.

Supplies of other than new buildings

A building remains 'new' for three years after practical completion or first occupation, whichever occurs first. Thereafter, any sale or lease follows different rules. *Domestic accommodation* can never be made taxable at standard rate; therefore, if it cannot be sold/leased at zero rate, it must be exempt. *All other buildings* will be exempt unless the option to tax is exercised. *Change of use* of qualifying building (i.e. zero-rated when new, other than domestic accommodation) within ten years of practical completion or first occupation, becomes a supply taxable at standard rate, which may result in the owner having to register (see Leaflet 708/4/89, Part IV). *The land itself* is taxable when sold or developed for new construction, unless one of the following notifications is given to the LVO:

● That rent for the new buildings (other than domestic or other qualifying buildings) will be taxed.

- That the developer will occupy the building himself for ten years.
- That the building will be sold within 3 years.

Undeveloped land will be exempt, unless the *option to tax* is exercised.

Option to tax

This must be exercised as soon as a new building is started, otherwise tax on the land itself will become chargeable. The option to tax existing leases can be exercised at any time, but related input tax cannot be reclaimed on supplies received earlier than 1 August 1989. Once exercised, the option to tax is irrevocable, until such time as the property is totally demolished or changes hands. All leases within a single building or complex must be either taxable or exempt (apart from domestic accommodation), but where the landlord owns a number of separate buildings or complexes, he may opt to tax specified buildings and not others (see Notice 742 B, Part V). Option to tax applies only to land and buildings for commercial use.

Ground rents and service charges

Generally follow the liability of the principal supply, except that where supplies are made individually to tenants (e.g. light, heat, power, ventilation) they will be taxable according to the nature of the supply *or* the status of the recipient, i.e. electricity will be zero rate to domestic accommodation, but standard rate to a business user.

Remember that this section on the taxing of land is not a full list of liabilities, but covers only the principal headings so that you will be aware of what lies in wait for you. The full liabilities on land, property and construction are to be found in the Vatman's notices and leaflets listed earlier in this chapter.

6 Second-hand goods and scrap

Introduction □ Special schemes □ Tax invoices □ Exports

Introduction

Second-hand goods, 'pre-owned' cars, old clothes, bits and pieces from the car-breaker, demolition materials ... And scrap – swarf, cullet, cabbage, off-cuts of timber, wastepaper, metal off-cuts and leftovers from stampings, retired office machines and furniture ... You can buy almost anything second-hand: a businessman recently advertised for a second-hand escalator! So why should there need to be any special arrangements for the VAT? Mostly, there aren't. Back in the days of purchase tax, *anything* second-hand or scrap (except precious metal) was tax-free. But under VAT, almost nothing second-hand is tax-free, unless it was zero-rated originally, like books. So, second-hand furniture for home or office; building materials from the demolition site; musical instruments; kitchen equipment (including cookers); cameras; tv sets; video recorders ... if it was standard rate 'new', it is standard rate 'used'. And one man's waste is another man's stock-in-trade – like the firm that picks up odds and ends of metal from an engineering works, sorts it and sells it. Wastepaper, waste oil, old clothes, glass bottles, aluminium cans – Steptoe & Son would have had to be registered! The rule is: if you sell it, tax it!

A word of warning on waste oil: *new* heating oil is zero rate because of its chemical and physical properties – but almost anything can be sold as 'burning oil', and that does not make it zero rate. Waste oil is always standard rate.

Special schemes

There are some goods which don't change hands once or twice, but are bought and sold many times; and some which are so expensive that even if they changed hands only a couple of times, the amount of VAT collected would be disproportionate. So, the 'special schemes' were devised to deal with them:

- Notice 711, *Cars*.
- Notice 712, *Antiques, art and collections*.
- Notice 713, *Motorcycles*.
- Notice 717, *Caravans*.
- Notice 720, *Boats and outboard motors*.
- Notice 721, *Aircraft*.
- Notice 722, *Electronic organs*.
- Notice 724, *Firearms*.
- Notice 726, *Horses*.

However, if any of these items end up as *scrap*, then VAT is chargeable on whatever price you get for them (a scrap horse . . .? The mind boggles!) If your second-hand goods or scrap do not fall within one of the special schemes, tax is chargeable on the full price.

Dealers

Anyone dealing in any of these items as a business, or as part of a business (a dealer in new cars, for instance, invariably has used cars for sale as well) is expected to use one of the special schemes – it is not compulsory, but you will soon see why it is a good idea.

No input tax is deductible on the purchase of a second-hand car, by a dealer or his customer, in any circumstances (or on any second-hand goods). VAT is charged on the 'margin', i.e. the amount by which the selling price exceeds the buying price, and any dealer who charged VAT on the full price would soon get an unmistakable message from his customers!

Records

The records required are rather more extensive than the basic purchase and sales records of ordinary traders. For each item of stock, the trader must record:

- Full details of the person from whom he bought the goods.
- A full description of the goods (for motor vehicles, this includes engine number, chassis number, licence plate number, and any changes made).
- Full details of the person to whom the goods are sold.
- Purchase price.

- Selling price.
- Margin.
- Rate and amount of VAT.

For cars, this runs to 19 columns: there are ready-printed stock books for just this purpose, produced by the motor trade. For the other classes of goods, the records are not quite so extensive, running to 15 columns. You can make up your own books, provided they contain all the necessary information. Except horses: there is a very special scheme for these and only the special forms produced by the British Equestrian Trade Association may be used.

Unless the records and procedures described in the notices are followed exactly, you will not be seen as using a special scheme and VAT on the full selling price will be called for, whether you have charged it or not.

Motor vehicles

By far the commonest second-hand scheme is for cars – and that means *cars*: sports cars and estate cars, cross-country vehicles, minibuses, crew buses, or any other passenger-vehicle with seats for less than 12 passengers (which excludes cars which are essentially pick-up trucks, vans, or other essentially goods vehicles). (See Notice 700, Appendix C and Notice 711 para. 2 for a definition of what constitutes a 'car'.)

Commercial vehicles

Vans, pick-ups, lorries of all descriptions, retired ambulances and anything which does not fulfil the legal requirements of a car, do not come within the second-hand scheme, and must be dealt with separately. VAT is chargeable (and deductible) on whatever price is charged.

Part-exchange

One of the commonest ways of getting a new car, whether it is 'new-new' or 'new-used', is to trade in the old one. The dealer's bill, after going through all manner of additions and subtractions, will come down to a final figure, which is what the buyer owes. This is not the figure on which VAT is calculated. The 'VAT figure' is the selling price of the 'new' car, and the final figure is only the settlement figure, after allowing for the trade-in value of the 'old' car. So, do not think that you are selling at a loss, and therefore do not have to account for any VAT, if the settlement figure is less than the purchase price of the new car! The Vatman could get quite annoyed at this and start working out assessments based on full selling prices, because you have failed to observe all the requirements of the special scheme!

Occasional sales and selling at a loss

Does this mean that any business which may, from time to time, sell the company car, get rid of the Managing Director's wife's favourite painting, or the messenger's motorbike . . . Do they have to go through all this rigmarole of recording who it was bought from, who it was sold to, and all the rest? Rest easy! The answer is, usually, no. Remember, VAT is to be accounted for on the mark-up of selling price over buying price, so if you sell at a loss, or even at the same price, there is no VAT accountable.

Dealers sometimes get caught with a nail, or maybe the manufacturer, anxious to shift old stock, will instruct the dealer to offer uneconomic trade-in values on old cars. In either case, the dealer is stuck with cars which he cannot sell at even the purchase price. Don't fret – if it is a genuine situation, there will be no VAT to account for. Even the Vatman gets Glass's *Guide* and can get a good idea of what Harry Bottle would have paid for that model in that condition.

Fleet operators

However, what about the business which buys cars by the fleet and get a very good discount, so that, when they come to sell off the old models a year or so later, the market value of those cars is in fact higher than the price they paid? Which could happen with car-hire operators, or a company with a large number of reps on the road. How would they go about disposing of the 'old' cars? Well, if they don't want to charge VAT on the full price of the 'old' cars, they must go through the complete scheme operation. The same applies to other goods which fall within one of the special schemes: either follow the scheme absolutely, or account for full-rate VAT. How much VAT? Not 15 per cent of the margin, but 3/23: the margin is taken as tax-inclusive.

Extras and expenses

Very few cars are resold without some work having been done on them, and the same general condition applies to all other special scheme goods. The cost of extras and expenses must not be added to the purchase price in order to reduce the margin and, thus, the amount of VAT to be accounted for. Obviously, the cost of work done will affect the selling price, and all VAT on the work done may be deducted – but output tax is the difference between buying and selling prices. Depending on precisely what goods are being sold, it is perfectly legal to invoice the customer separately for extras or work done: the output tax will be the same in the end.

Antiques, works of art and collectors' pieces

This scheme makes no artistic judgment!

Antiques

If an object is more than 100 years old, it is an antique and can be sold under the scheme. But the age of 100 years at the time of selling is *absolute*: pity the lady who thought of setting up a 'period dress' business and found that most of her stock counted simply as old clothes! Or the militaria dealer who had two identical bayonets – identical, that is, except for the year of manufacture embossed in the steel. At the date in question, one was an antique and the other was not! The silly thing was that the other one became an antique a year later!

Breaking up

If an item is bought and then broken up and sold piecemeal (a book, for instance, which is virtually unsellable but which contains pictures which, trimmed and mounted, are highly sellable), the records required are still exactly the same. VAT is still accountable on the mark-up of selling price over purchase price, and if, by the time the purchase price has been divided among the pieces, the mark-up is practically the whole of the selling price, you might be better off dealing with the pieces outside the scheme anyway. Not included in the scheme are pearls and other loose gemstones (i.e. precious stones, not semi-precious).

Works of art

It can be anything. Literally, anything. Provided it is 'art', executed in any material, and is the original work and not a mechanical copy (a copy executed by hand may be includable), it can be handled within the scheme. Age does not count. Not included is the first sale of the item by the artist or previously unsold items forming part of his estate (i.e. there must have been at least one other owner between the artist and the current sale).

Collections

Not just any old collection of bits and pieces, no matter how interesting or fascinating the collector found them, but something of scientific, social, historical or ethnic importance. Age and artistic merit don't matter. Notice 712 gives quite an extensive list of what qualifies and what doesn't.

Occasional sales

As for all other schemes, the full requirements must be observed, or VAT is chargeable on the full selling price. Stately home sales may either be exempt (see Leaflet 701/39, *Exempt Group 11*), or taxable if the items formed part of a display or exhibition for public viewing (see Leaflet 701/12, *Sales from Stately Homes*).

Private sales

The selling of private property which has never been 'on view' as part of a tourist or trade attraction – like the contents of a stately home – does not attract VAT even if the sale goes well over the registration figure. However, if qualifying items which are privately owned are brought into the business as stock, VAT will become chargeable. And since the purchase price will be nil, the mark-up will be the whole price. But it will still count as a second-hand scheme sale, with all that that implies.

Tax invoices

Tax invoices are not to be issued. For goods sold under one of the second-hand schemes, it is a condition that no input tax will be deducted by either the dealer or his customer, so a tax invoice is not to be issued – just a bill of sale. If the customer insists on a tax invoice, because it is a business purchase, let him insist: you can't do it. And refer him to the LVO.

Exports

Follow the general rules for exports (Notices 703 and 704) and remember that your displayed selling price is normally *tax inclusive*. And exports are zero rate . . . That's right – you make a bit extra on exports! But be warned: usually, you will have to export the goods direct and not deliver them to the customer in the UK (this applies especially to motor vehicles). Contact your LVO for approval if a customer wants to export a used motor vehicle of any sort. Alternatively, treat it as an ordinary taxable sale and let the customer do what he likes. However, if you choose to knock off a bit for a zero rate export, it means *you* must control the export. (See Chapter 7.)

6

7 Imports and exports

Introduction □ Imports and goods in bond □ Import of services □ Exports □ Retail exports □ Direct export □ Export of services □ Re-imports

Introduction

Don't say that you'll never get involved with imports and exports! The day you say that, you can bet your boots you'll find that the only place to get left-handed panic-bolts is Mexico City and you've got a customer who must have some. Or only your stock of double-jointed bricklayer's hods is suitable for rebuilding an earthquake-devastated village in Central Uttar Panspeci.

Don't laugh and say, 'It couldn't happen to *me!*' – because it could. The world is a very small place these days, and you are probably wearing a shirt made in South Korea, shoes from Yugoslavia and socks from Taiwan. As for where electronic goods come from . . . Even food is flown in from some unlikely places: during Bob Geldof's campaign to get aid to thousands of people dying of starvation in Ethiopia, we were shipping whisky by the shipload to them, and they were sending salad stuff to us! It can happen. So be prepared at least in knowing that procedures exist for moving stuff between countries and accounting for the VAT.

Imports and goods in bond

Imports are probably easier to handle than exports – you don't have to rely on someone else sending you evidence of movement – you get it for yourself. (See Notice 702 and Leaflets 702/1,2,3,4.) For a long time, a registered trader did not have to pay VAT at importation, but had to account for it in the VAT return. This, like so many concessions, was abused, so now everyone has to pay VAT before getting their hands on the goods.

Postal imports

These have already been mentioned in Chapter 3: provided your

VAT number is quoted on the outside of the parcel, together with the value, then up to £1,300 can still be handled by 'postponed accounting' (i.e. the amount of VAT assessed on the import value is to be entered in your VAT account as *VAT due but not paid*). At the same time, input tax may be claimed on the other side of the VAT account, to the extent that it may be claimed. This means that if the goods are not for use wholly within the business or, for some other reason, the VAT cannot be claimed in its entirety (for instance, if it relates directly to an exempt output), then you claim only the amount to which you are entitled. This is where some of the tax may stick. Without your VAT number on the outside of the packet, you will have to pay the VAT before you can get your goods, as you will also have to do for packets exceeding £1,300 value. Naturally, you must keep all import documents, Post Office notices and labels, etc. to prove your claim to input tax.

What would happen if you ignored the VAT on both sides of the VAT account? Not a lot, but a visiting Vatman might assess you for the missing output tax (plus penalty and interest) which would not be entirely offset by the input tax you would then claim. If too many people did that, it could distort our overall national VAT bill, which would affect our contribution to the EC budget, and we could be assessed for a greater percentage contribution which was unnecessary . . . for the want of a nail.

Other imports

Imports can come in through any port or airport, and all are assessed for duty and VAT and, basically, the customs charges must be paid before you can get your hands on them.

Occasional imports

If you make only occasional imports, it is virtually certain that you will have to pay hard cash before you get your goods, which means either being there in person, or appointing an agent to do it for you – and he will charge you for doing it, especially for financing the VAT. Fortunately, there will be no VAT on his charges. If, for instance, you or an employee make an occasional trip to France or Spain and come back with a load of pottery, or fabrics, or even booze, it may pay you to have cash or a certified cheque on you to clear customs with the shortest delay – otherwise, you could wait for a day or more!

Regular imports

Engage an agent: they know the procedures backwards. Some of them are even ex-customs officers who know (or should know) both sides of the procedure. And, furthermore, you can almost revert to postponed accounting! It is now called 'deferred accounting' and in fact requires you to deposit, or arrange a guarantee of, a fixed sum of money, usually under the control of your agent, to be paid to customs periodically. Of course, you cannot claim input tax until you receive the customs print-out of your individual imports and VAT payments. Please, don't anticipate input tax on imports, any more than you would on other purchases. If a visiting Vatman finds that you have, he may well issue an assessment simply in order to raise the penalty and interest on the use of money to which you were not entitled at the time. Wait for the Vatman's valuation before you claim the VAT.

There are other aspects to imports, of course, which are explained in Notice 702, but these will rarely affect the smaller, occasional importer.

Agents

By far the best advice for any importer, regular or occasional, is: find a good import agent. Ports and airports are surrounded by them.

Goods in bond

Customs officers hardly ever refer to 'goods in bond'. They will refer to a 'bonded warehouse', and goods therein will be known as 'warehoused goods'. Some bonded warehouses are no more than a section of an ordinary warehouse, unenclosed, unsealed, unprotected in any way except by the warehouse keeper's 'contract' with Customs and Excise. Others, like whisky warehouses, are securely locked and under the supervision of a customs officer. But, whatever the physical form, the goods within are duty- and tax-free, and only dutiable goods can be warehoused.

Dutiable goods produced within the UK and warehoused, like whisky, are treated in exactly the same way as imports when they are taken out of bond for home use: they will be valued for duty and VAT and you won't get them until you've paid up. This does not mean that you cannot buy and sell warehoused goods. You can buy and sell them, duty- and tax-free, and they never leave the warehouse! They can be sold a dozen times, with never a penny of duty or tax being levied – but the person who finally takes them out of bond will have to pay up all the duty and VAT on their value at the day they are removed.

Quayside sales

Goods can also be bought and sold on the quayside before they have been 'entered' for home use, or even before the ship has docked, or the plane landed. Such sales are specifically zero-rated under the terms of Zero Rate Sch. Group 15 Item 1, and the person who finally makes the customs entry will be responsible for duty and VAT.

Duty

Never forget that duty may be payable on some goods, is not deductible, and that VAT is calculated on the value *plus* duty. There are a lot of customs notices about various aspects of importation, or specific goods being imported, all free from the customs office. There is also a massive volume known as *The Tariff*, which lists just about every piece of goods produced anywhere in the world and what its rate of duty is. This is not handed out free, but you can telephone and ask for the duty on your particular goods.

7

Carriage

I have said that the import agent's fees are VAT-free, which is because they are services in connection with imports, in a customs port or airport. Carriage of goods is entirely different. The carriage of goods to or from a port or airport is taxable at standard rate, but 'through transport' is zero rate (i.e. where the goods travel from your supplier right to your shop or warehouse, on the same vehicle). The same applies to goods travelling from your stores right through to the overseas customer. But as soon as goods are transhipped for carriage in the UK, the carriage becomes taxable.

Import of services

The export of services is zero rate, but those same services, when imported, become taxable. The following are known as the 'Schedule 3' services:

● Transfer of copyright etc.
● Advertising.

- Services of consultants (non-medical).
- *Not* doing something for payment.
- Banking and finance.
- Supply of staff.
- Hiring goods.
- Insurance.

Any of these services, received by a registered person in the UK, is taxable. Although there are no forms, you must record the value of the imported service, calculate VAT at 15 per cent and declare it in your VAT account as *tax due but not paid* on the outputs side, and at the same time, deduct as much as you are allowed.

The notices call it 'reverse charge' on imported services, but treat it like a postal import; assess the VAT yourself, handle it as 'postponed accounting', and you'll probably get it right. If you are in any doubt, contact your LVO and get written confirmation. (See Zero Rate Sch. Group 9, *International Services* and Notice 741.)

Exports

There are two ways of getting goods out of the country: as a 'normal' or 'direct' export (see Notice 703 and Leaflets 703/1,2,3), or as a retail 'over-the-counter' export (see Notice 704 and Leaflets 704/1,2). For dealers in *new* motor vehicles, there is Notice 705, *Personal Export of New Motor Vehicles*.

There is one overriding rule for exports: to qualify for zero rating, *you* must hold the evidence of export, and *you* must be able to show that the named goods were exported.

Retail exports

'Retail export' means that the overseas customer takes the goods with him from your shop, just like any other customer. However, you cannot be compelled to operate the scheme: it is entirely voluntary, and if you do choose to operate it, you can set your own limits on what you will sell under the scheme (say, nothing under £100, or whatever price makes it economic to operate). If you are in a heavily-foreign-tourist-infested area, then it may be economic not to set a limit, but you can still make a charge for administration and relieve the customer of, say, 12.5 per cent instead of the full 15 per cent (or whatever you reckon is a fair deduction for administration expenses).

Rules

If you decide to operate the scheme, there are certain rules, both as to the goods and the customer, and of course, the records. For a start, there is a form, the VAT 407, obtainable from your LVO. From a VAT point of view, there is no restriction on what can be dealt with under retail export – excepting only motor vehicles and boats, goods sent direct to a foreign address, and business sales. But there is a restriction on what can be sold, based on very practical considerations. If the customer is leaving the country by air, the goods must be able to be carried as *cabin luggage*. For anyone leaving by ship, the goods can be larger. In either case, however, they must not be packed in luggage, nor in sealed packages, because they have to be presented to customs, either on leaving the country, or on arrival at the other end. For EC travellers, proof of export from Britain is provided by proof of import into the country of destination. For all other travellers, proof of export must be obtained at the port or airport of departure.

Notice 704 does give quite clear instructions on what must appear on the form, and how to account for goods, VAT and administrative expenses, but there is no mention of the restrictions imposed by the airlines.

Oversize goods

If the customer wants to take the goods as baggage-hold luggage, he must allow sufficient time before flight departure to present the goods to customs, repack his luggage and then hand it in at the check-in.

Monetary limits

There is a special feature for EC travellers. Depending on which country they are from, there is a value restriction on what can be handled under the scheme: £45 for Eire, £145 for Greece, and £163 for the rest of the EC (see Leaflet 704/1). Up to these values, the traveller pays full VAT in the UK, gets no refund, but pays no more on entry to his own country. Which will undoubtedly change in 1992: very probably, there will be no distinction between UK customers and EC travellers. No matter which country anyone is in, they will simply be treated as an ordinary customer, buying their goods tax-inclusive and simply taking them home, with no more to pay on entry to their home country.

Obtaining proof of export

You can, if you wish, sell your goods tax-free and hope that the customer will send back the form; but if he doesn't, then guess what? The Vatman takes the VAT off you anyway. The more usual method is to charge VAT to start with and to send a refund when you get that form back. For other than EC travellers, you are expected to provide a stamped, addressed envelope, so that, when a UK customs officer has certified the export, he can pop the form in the envelope and send it straight back to you. Customs and Excise are not expected or required to supply envelope and postage for your export forms, so if you don't provide envelope and postage you probably won't get evidence of export – and you will get a bad reputation among foreign visitors. For community travellers, provide the addressed envelope, and rely on them to put the proper postage on it in their own country.

Alternative evidence

Customs certification is the best evidence, of course. However, say that through cussedness, force of circumstances, or carelessness (the stuff was packed in the luggage and so was not seen by a customs officer), the best evidence was not obtained: Notice 704 describes what alternative evidence may be accepted – and if satisfactory evidence is not obtained, zero rating cannot be allowed. (An unscrupulous trader zero-rated his retail exports in the accounts and pocketed the refunds. Overseas customers complained, but there was little that could be done: he had the certified forms and evidence that refunds had been sent; so, if those incompetent/crooked foreign postal services didn't deliver the refunds – what could he do . . .? Until he zero-rated some uncertified exports: he had the forms, but no satisfactory evidence of export. Then the Vatman could lean on him, and the message was simple: either refund the VAT, or pay it to the Vatman. Most of it was refunded.)

Accounts

The sale will initially go through your accounts as an ordinary taxable sale. If the Form 407 hasn't come back by the end of the tax period, don't worry: declare your sales at the full rate of VAT. When the form does come back, and you make the refund (adjusted for any administration charges), simply make a credit entry in the outputs, cross-referenced to the export form(s). (The best way would be to have a separate section of your VAT account for 'export refunds'.) Having calculated your output tax on the full, tax-inclusive price, enter the refunds made on the 407s received back in that period. You don't have to tie up each individual export with each individual refund simply for the purposes of the VAT return − but a visiting Vatman may require a match.

A cumbersome system? Well, maybe. But it is easier to do than to describe. Read through the notice a couple of times, perhaps work out a procedure list, and you will undoubtedly find that, in operation, it is relatively simple. But do remember:

- Only you can refund the VAT.
- There is no way in which Customs and Excise can make the refund.

Although it is not all uncommon for someone to do the rounds of the shops, carefully collect all the bills of sale, and then, from the depths of the Congo basin or the Nullabor plain, send them all to customs HQ with a note saying, 'Please send me the VAT on this lot'. Sorry, no way!

How to make the refund

Notice 704 says that you must agree on how to make the refund. Basically, you will need an International Money Order, convertible into the customer's currency, in his home country. A cheque in pounds and pence may present difficulties at the other end, especially with fluctuating exchange rates. If you will be doing it regularly, consult your bank manager or local post office supervisor and set up a system that any employee can follow.

Non-entitled persons

The over-the-counter scheme cannot be used by the crews of ships or aircraft, or by UK residents (and 'resident' is not confined to citizens, but includes diplomats, visiting forces, students, employees of overseas companies, actors, anyone, in fact, who has been in the country for more than 24 months continuously). They can still obtain zero-rated export, but cannot take the goods with them. For those leaving by ship, there is a different form, VAT 435, (which involves *you* sending the goods to the ship, or to the ship's agent) to be produced to customs. Do not send the stuff to the Custom House: it will not be accepted and may well miss the boat, literally – and there goes one more disappointed customer. You should still not sell the goods tax-free, or make a refund, until that form is back in your hands, certified as to export. Residents leaving by air *cannot* get zero-rating this way: the airlines simply cannot handle the traffic. Nor can they use the 407 system. The only alternative is a **direct export** to their overseas address (see below). If postage/shipping charges work out to more than the VAT, they may just have to grin and bear it, pay the VAT and take the goods with them.

Groupage

There is one other course open to anyone leaving the country – resident, EC traveller or complete foreigner. If he is buying a number of items, from different shops, it may well be more convenient for him to have all the separate purchases sent to an **export packer** – *sent*, not taken – and the packer will provide the evidence of export, but not under the retail schemes: the customer may not take delivery of goods in the UK.

Finally, don't forget that retail export schemes can be used only by retailers. A trade export, where the customer takes the stuff with him, requires quite different documentation (see Notice 703).

Direct export

Here, once again, *you* must control the export. You may know perfectly well that the goods you supply to the place down the road will be exported, but unless you control the export, you cannot claim zero-rating. The general rule is: if goods are delivered to a customer in the UK, zero-rating cannot apply. But having said that, there are a couple of exceptions. (For direct export and export packers, see Notice 703.)

Delivery to an export packer

This has already been mentioned in 'Retail exports', and means just what it says: an export packer specialises in packing goods for export and usually also trundles them round to the port or airport of departure and obtains the 'bill of lading', 'air weighbill', or an acceptable equivalent – a copy of which must then be delivered to you. Without that document, the Vatman will call for VAT on the goods even if you have not charged any.

Export houses

These are a peculiar animal: they have no trading stock of their own, but will arrange for almost anything to be exported. They may also have their own packing department, but they are not export packers. The way an export house works is this: they have an overseas customer who wants a load of glassware, kitchen utensils and door knockers; they will have to go to different suppliers in the UK to fill the order. For each UK supplier to operate zero-rating, he must either send the goods direct to the port of departure, or to an export packer. If the goods are delivered to the export house's own packing department, zero-rating does *not* apply, and it counts as a standard rate supply to the export house, not as a zero-rated export to the overseas customer.

Export in luggage

Your overseas customer may want to take the goods with him, especially if they are small enough, or of high value (which usually means small size as well), or can be packed in a motor vehicle (which invariably means he is leaving by sea). You can zero-rate the supply provided you can guarantee to get evidence of export by way of a bill of lading, air weighbill or equivalent; otherwise, take a deposit of VAT, rather like a retail export. There is no VAT form for trade exports: you must obtain evidence of export by normal commercial documentation.

Groupage and consolidation

If your goods are to be incorporated in other goods (consolidation), or packed with other goods before export (groupage), you can still zero-rate your supply to someone in the UK, provided you get from him a copy of the ultimate export document for all the goods. Or you can treat the supply as an ordinary taxable supply within the UK and let him handle zero-rating for export. The particular records you must keep are described in Notice 703: basically, you must be able to tie up each export sale with its own export documents.

Own exports

It might be, of course, that you ship the goods out yourself, by air, sea, or post. Anyone making regular exports will either have their own export department, or will use a shipping agent. There are no VAT forms, don't forget, so you must prove zero-rating to a visiting Vatman with commercial documentation. This also applies to exports by road vehicle leaving the country by ferry, British Rail parcels service, or independent carrier.

Occasional exports

If you have only occasional exports, your best bet is to find an export agent, shipping agent, or packer and let him take the strain. He will charge for his services, of course, but you may find that preferable to treading strange ground yourself. And you can always add an administration charge to your bill!

Exports to British embassies etc.

Goods must be delivered to the Foreign and Commonwealth Office for delivery to overseas missions by diplomatic bag or freight, and a certificate of shipment must be obtained from them. Contact the FCO baggage room before you start sending large packing cases of stuff!

Supplies to the armed forces

The MOD is constantly shifting goods in and out of the country and it would be an impossible job to 'export' every round of ammunition and pair of socks, and then to 'import' them on return. Therefore, all supplies to the MOD are counted as taxable, inland deliveries, even if delivered to a military port and you see the stuff loaded aboard a military transport – you do not control the export.

Exports to members of the armed forces

Private exports to servicemen serving abroad, or their families, must either be done by Form VAT 453 (see 'Retail Exports' above) or alternative proof of export must be obtained from the military police at the purchaser's place of duty (see Notice 704).

Supplies to foreign missions

Goods for use within the mission, within the UK, are not exports, but goods for onward shipment to the home country are exports, provided you get a certificate of export. If foreign diplomats or the staff of High Commissions insist that they should get their purchases at zero rate, *do not give in*. Should they be entitled to tax relief, they can claim a refund through the Protocol Department of the FCO – but they must pay first!

Visiting forces

Some visiting forces, particularly US and NATO, can get tax relief on some goods – usually, for use within their military enclave, *or* for 'consumer durables' for private use, such as cookers, refrigerators and the like. In either case, the purchaser must produce an official order, signed by an authorised official and quoting a British Customs and Excise reference number. And it must be consumer durables, not like the junior officer from an eastern mission who tried to deck his wife out in cheap imitation jewellery when the authorised officer was on leave and he had access to the purchase orders! It came as quite a shock to him to discover that the local Vatman simply would not authorise the shopkeeper to zero-rate the sale!

7

Postal exports

Obtain a certificate of posting, either on the Post Office's own form, or on customs form C & E 132, obtainable from the Collector's Office, *not* the VAT office. For high value goods and goods requiring a customs declaration, there is the 'export label', VAT 444, obtainable from the LVO.

Motor vehicles

All other goods must be exported virtually immediately. Retail exports must leave the country within three months. But new cars can stay in the country for up to one year, after which they may be seized and full payment of duty and VAT will be demanded on the *new* price. Export is arranged only by the factory or main agent – the local Ford or Honda dealer can't do it, except by going through the main agent. If a customer wants a tax-free car, either refer him to the factory or main agent, or contact your LVO, who in turn should be able to contact the main agent.

If a customer wants to export a second-hand vehicle, get advice from your LVO. Generally, *you* will have to arrange direct export: the customer cannot take delivery in the UK.

Ships or aircraft stores

Supplies to shipping or aircraft companies, for distribution to their vessels, are *not* exports and must be taxed according to the nature of the goods. Stores supplied directly on board ship or aircraft are exports, provided a certificate is given by the ship's master, owner or authorised agent. Mess and canteen stores for HM ships may be zero-rated in the same way, notwithstanding that supplies to the MOD cannot be zero-rated.

Full details are in Notices 702, 703 and 704. For anything that is not clear, get positive instructions from your LVO. Hopefully, the foregoing will point you in the right direction if import or export questions do come your way.

Export of services

There are no forms for this (see Leaflet 701/39, Zero Rate Sch. Group 11, *International Services*). To qualify for zero-rating, you must be able to show that the principal beneficiary of your services is outside the UK. This may sometimes be difficult where the beneficiary has an establishment within the UK, and the UK office may make the payment. You should have sufficient documentation to show that your services were ordered by someone outside the country and were delivered outside the country. If you make a written report, for instance, which is delivered to the UK establishment, it will be very difficult to prove that the principle beneficiary is a foreign customer. But if the business is operating in the UK, it will almost certainly be registered, so it will do no harm to charge VAT – which they can deduct. What they do internally is then none of your concern. Even if it does not conduct business in the UK, it should still be registered, precisely for this purpose: to buy goods and services for transmission to the home office, free of VAT.

Re-imports

If you are sending goods out of the country, which will be brought back within a few months (e.g. exhibition goods, goods sent for overhaul or repair, tools and equipment to perform some service or process outside the country, etc.), be sure to declare your intention to customs *before* you go, or before you send the goods. It will make it so much easier to get the goods back into the UK without being charged VAT and duty. (Provided you kept the declaration and had it stamped by customs! Contact the local Excise office for details.)

7

8 Dealing with officialdom

Visits by the Vatman □ After the visit □ Disputes □ Appeals □ After the tribunal □ Official powers □ Assessment, penalties and interest □ Selling to official bodies

Visits by the Vatman

Up to now, we have talked about the 'Vatman', which, indeed, is how many people refer to him, but his proper title is Officer of Customs and Excise, and you are as likely to be visited by a female officer as by a man. There are four grades of officer who might visit you:

- Officer (general civil service grade EO – Executive Officer).
- Senior Officer (HEO – Higher Executive Officer).
- Surveyor (SEO – Senior Executive Officer).
- Assistant Collector (Principal).

Mostly it will be an officer or a senior officer; sometimes there will be two of them: a senior officer checking on the work of an officer, or a surveyor checking on a senior officer or officer, or an assistant collector checking on any one of the other three. If your books or business are very complicated, you may get a team of senior officer and officer as a regular matter. You should never have more than two – unless it's a raid by the Investigation Branch waving a search warrant! (See Leaflet 700/26.)

Myths

Let's put a few myths and rumours where they belong. A visiting Vatman cannot demand money from you: even if you know and he knows that you are in arrears, he cannot demand money. He can issue you with various notices to pay, but if you don't want to pay him there and then, that's the end of the matter. (It's different if he calls with a bailiff, of course, but even then, it won't come out of the blue: you will have had plenty of warning!) He cannot break in, except with a warrant and in the presence of a policeman. He cannot demand entry at an unreasonable hour, and once in, he cannot search without a search warrant.

Have you heard of the 'VAT Gestapo'? It happened like this. It was an antique dealer who was on the fiddle, defrauding the revenue, and a team from the Investigation Branch raided his premises one morning, with a search warrant and a policeman. It was about 9 a.m. That's right – nine o'clock in the morning. The local press reported the raid, describing it as carried out 'with all the efficiency of the Gestapo making a midnight raid', in the usual over-the-top style of local press. Without checking, the national press picked up the story of 'the VAT Gestapo making a midnight raid'.

Another myth is that the Vatman can take money off you; but, whether you owe it or not, he can't. His job is to protect the revenue, and to that end he can demand that you pay every penny that is legally due – and not a penny more – though sometimes a few pennies less. Customs and Excise officers are allowed a certain degree of discretion and may waive small amounts of tax, while insisting that you account for it in future. Under certain circumstances, quite large amounts of tax can be waived by collectors and commissioners, if there are good reasons for doing so. Basically, you must be able to show that you were misdirected by an officer of Customs and Excise, or that the published instructions were unclear or ambiguous. It is no good saying you were misdirected by your accountant or the bloke next door! You'll have to pay up, and sue your accountant!

Timing the visit

OK, that's who he is and what he can't do. What can he do, when, and how often? Can he just knock at the door and walk in and demand to see everything? Strictly speaking – yes he can. He has the authority to enter, at a reasonable time, any premises where business is being conducted, and to inspect the premises, the business, the goods and the records. However, routine VAT inspections are not carried out in that way. Your first visit after registration will come up in 15 – 18 months. An officer of Customs and Excise will telephone you, identify themself and ask to make an appointment to look at your business and your books. This first visit should not take more than half a day, as a rule (it can go on longer, of course, if there are complications). All future visits will be arranged the same way: phone call first.

However, if you cancel the appointment, put him off, are absent when he calls, don't have the books ready, the Vatman will appoint another date to suit *him*, and a couple more failures to allow the inspection, or failures to produce the books, will result in a notice to produce your records. If you ignore that, you start clocking up a penalty of £5 a day until you do produce. This is the worst case, of course, and if you have a reasonable excuse for not keeping the appointment – for instance, illness in the family, your business takes you abroad or to the other end of the country, even that you've booked your holidays for the time the Vatman wants to call – the Vatman will normally come to some mutually convenient date. Once or twice! After a couple of deferments, a reasonable excuse becomes unreasonable!

The day arrives

What will the Vatman want to see? Who will he want to see? Certainly on the first visit, he will want to talk to the person in charge, the boss, the registered person, a partner or a director. No matter that he will spend most of his time with the bookkeeper or the accountant, he will want a few words with the boss first. He will want details of the business, your financial year, the name and address of your accountant and/or auditor. He will discuss what, exactly, the business does and how it does it: he will want to chart the flow of orders, materials and money through the business; know how instructions are given to workshop staff; see where the various bits of paper are stored, and what accounting system you have.

The premises

He may ask to have a look round, to inspect the place. He cannot *search*, remember, although he may ask what is behind that door, or what is kept in those boxes, and an unwillingness to tell or show him could rouse his suspicions enough to bring him back with a search warrant – provided he can persuade his assistant collector and a magistrate! If you conduct your business from your private house, he cannot demand to inspect the domestic accommodation: he is restricted to premises where business is conducted. This does not exclude, however, the 'domestic offices' of business premises.

The goods

If you deal in goods – from thimbles to oil rigs – he may ask to inspect the storerooms: you cannot refuse. If the business involves dangerous substances, or ultra-clean rooms, or livestock, or sensitive or secret material, he is required to observe sensible precautions. A good Vatman has his eyes open all the time!

The records

Having determined what the business does, the Vatman will then turn to how it is all recorded – in other words, the books and invoices, orders, credit notes, import and export documents, production orders, despatch notes, expenses, etc. Anything which has a bearing on the business, on the money, and therefore on the tax, he may ask to see. He needs to be satisfied that your VAT return is a credible document and that all your business, and tax, is reflected there. Remember, the law requires that you keep records from which you can calculate your tax liability, and from which an authorised person can check your workings.

Basically, the Vatman will want to check how the figures get to the VAT account, on both sides, and where the money went. So you will have to have on hand not only your books of account, but also your annual accounts, your banking records (a court ruling many years ago decreed that the banking records were part of the financial records which an authorised person could demand to see), copy invoices (a retailer has input invoices, don't forget), till readings . . . the whole shooting match. Not forgetting your VAT registration certificate and company certificate of incorporation (if you are a limited company).

How long

It has already been said that a first visit would not normally take longer than half a day – so, how can a Vatman check all this stuff in half a day? You will know perfectly well how long your accountant takes to go through things and reach a trial balance. Of course the Vatman will not go through everything in the course of a visit, but it must be there in case he decides that, *this* time, he will look at *this* aspect.

The end of the visit

When he has finished with your books etc., the Vatman may want to speak to you again, to clear up any queries, to advise you of pitfalls, to answer any questions. If he has found any errors in your records, he won't keep it to himself! You will be asked for explanations as he finds the errors. If it is a case of straightforward cock-ups, he may tell you that he will be sending an assessment – he can't issue it on the spot because it has to go through the 'system' and be recorded. If it is something more complicated, he will probably tell you that he will lay it all out in a letter and that you will have time to dig up an explanation. This is often the case when, for instance, your turnover declared in the VAT returns is noticeably less than the turnover shown in the accounts: invariably, you'll need your accountant's help here.

After April 1990, there may be a nasty shock in store for some traders when it comes to assessments, penalties and interest: if you have found an error in earlier periods, other than the permitted £1,000, and have corrected it in a later period, the Vatman can call for interest, for the time the tax was missing, even though there is no net tax now owing!

If he does not find a mistake because he didn't look at that aspect of the business this time, it does not mean that it's OK for all time: the next visiting Vatman might turn it up and trace arrears of tax right back to the day you started!

After the visit

Do you have any complaints? Did the Vatman behave as he should have? If you believe that there was anything improper about the visiting Vatman's behaviour, you must write immediately to his assistant collector. It's no use leaving it a few weeks and then write some vague objection: do it at once, with all the detail you can recall. This includes not only objectionable behaviour to you, your employees, visitors or family, but also incompetent behaviour – especially if it leads to an improper assessment, or you consider that he was wasting taxpayers' money. (Did he leave at noon, and you found him sunbathing in the meadow at 4 p.m.? Let his bosses know.)

When will he be back?

After leaving you, the Vatman will have to write a report, both verbal for his superiors, and in code for the computer: are your records good, complicated, computerised, a mess? Are you careful, a good organiser, or is your business chaotic? How reliable are your VAT returns?

His coding, plus your performance as recorded by the computer from your returns, will determine how soon he will back. It could be anything from half a day in eight years, down to a couple of days a month, but for the majority of businesses it will be a day, perhaps two, every two or three years. Or a day or two every year, depending very much on the size of the business.

Visits out of sequence

However, just because the Vatman's been and gone, it doesn't mean that he might not come back sooner. The computer at Southend is programmed to pick out VAT returns that are unusual – for instance, a regular payer who suddenly puts in a repayment claim for many thousands of pounds. The return will be sent to your LVO for investigation and chances are you will get a 'miscellaneous' visit for the sole purpose of checking on that one return. (Did you buy an expensive new machine or heavy lorry or something? Rebuild the shop, invest in diamonds or something? Provided it was a legitimate business expense, there will be no problem. But you would not, for instance, be allowed to claim for the major refurbishment of a building which is let out on an exempt rent.)

Other reasons for calls out of sequence could be a sudden drop in turnover or a change in turnover value which is not matched by an increase in output tax. And, of course, failure to submit returns. In this case, you will be visited by a member of the enforcement team, and ultimately by a bailiff – but it's already been said: in this situation, the visit won't be entirely unexpected!

8

Repayment traders

Incidentally, repayment traders who do not send in returns are not chased: they are not withholding tax, and they are penalising themselves. But they will still get the routine visit, and if it turns out that they should have been paying tax on the missing returns . . . well, the Vatman will get his assessment forms out.

Disputes

Mostly, traders who get an assessment recognise that they owe the money. They may not like paying the extra, but they accept it. However, there is always the case where you may disagree with the assessment for any of a variety of reasons: the Vatman didn't take sufficient information into account; you consider the amount excessive; you disagree with his interpretation of your supplies and reckon they should be zero rate; you consider that you should be allowed to deduct that item of input tax. There could be as many reasons as there are registered traders and officers of Customs and Excise!

It might not be a matter of assessment: it could be your effective date of registration; the liability of left-handed panic bolts labelled in braille which you say are fully printed items; or the value of stocks and assets at the date of deregistration . . . In fact, just about anything where you dispute the Vatman's ruling or decision.

Whatever the basis for your disagreement, your first step is to ask the Vatman you are dealing with to reconsider his action. This might escalate into an appeal, so you need all the evidence you can get. If you conduct any part of your dispute by telephone, take a note of the date and time, try to get the name of the person you are speaking to (if you don't already know who it is – i.e. you might have asked for 'your' Vatman specifically and you are in no doubt about his identity), take a note of what was said and, if possible, have a witness at your end of the phone. If the matter goes to appeal and the LVO denies that it ever had a phone call from you, and your witness is a close family member, the appeal tribunal may not place much weight on the evidence. Of course, if you have an answerphone that can record a two-way conversation . . . Usually, though, in cases of uncertainty, you will have been sent a letter to start with, setting out the situation and asking for your explanation.

A motor dealer disputed an assessment: his annual accounts showed £6,000 more business than his VAT returns did, so he was assessed for 3/23 of that figure after being given an opportunity to explain the difference. His only 'explanation' was that he had done jolly well to get the two figures to agree so closely . . . The assessment stuck. The officer is obliged to report such cases to his superiors, and, in fact, to discuss it with them. If they agree with him, he will tell you that the matter has been re-examined, and that his decision stands. But this is not the end.

Appeals

You can take your dispute to the VAT tribunal, which is independent of Customs and Excise, although its office staff are seconded from Customs and Excise as being more likely to understand the content of the papers they handle. The tribunal itself is composed of independent lawyers. They are not judges, merely members of the tribunal. If you decide to go to appeal, there are two sets of circumstances you must take note of:

- Is the matter appealable?
- Is it in time?

Appealable matters

The LVO carries a stock of appeal notices and forms and will hand them out free, but for quick reference, these are the only appealable matters:

- An assessment or the amount of an assessment.
- Registration or cancellation of registration.
- Refusal to allow a group registration or a change in group registration.
- Refusal to allow exemption from registration or to allow voluntary registration.
- The tax chargeable on a supply of goods or services or the importation of goods.
- The amount of deductible input tax.
- The apportionment of taxable and exempt supplies.
- Refund of tax to a DIY housebuilder.
- Refund of tax on a bad debt.
- Refund of VAT on the importation of another person's private property.
- A direction as to open market value.
- Refusal to allow the use of a retail scheme.
- A requirement regarding computer-produced invoices.
- Requiring security for tax payable.
- A penalty or surcharge.
- The amount of penalty, surcharge or interest.
- A direction that two or more persons shall be registered as a single person (anti-disaggregation).

Timetable

Basically, the appeal must be lodged within 30 days of the date of the letter or notice containing the disputed matter. Which means, of course, that you cannot appeal against a verbal direction or bad behaviour. All of the above matters will be notified to you by letter or official form or notice (e.g. an assessment on a form in the VAT 600 series). You can go about things in one of two ways:

1. You can go straight to tribunal with your appeal;
2. You can ask your LVO to review the matter first.

But you must make the first move within those 30 days.

As soon as an appeal is lodged, the Vatman himself is tied to a timetable: an officer, normally at least two grades above the officer who issued the letter or notice, must review the matter and decide whether it was a good decision, i.e. whether it was properly made, on the correct grounds and by the correct procedures. If the reviewing officer thinks the decision was good and should stand, he will notify the tribunal and if you decide that, even so, you will pursue the appeal, a hearing date will be set. After that, it's a matter for the tribunal alone. If the reviewing officer disagrees with the decision, either in principle or degree, you will be informed that the decision has been withdrawn, or the amount of tax etc. involved reduced.

Gaining time

Alternatively, you can notify your LVO that you intend to appeal, but would like a local review first. They are then obliged to send you a letter stating that when the review is complete, you will be sent a further letter giving a date from which you will have 30 days to lodge an appeal with the tribunal. This gives both sides more time to consider their positions and gather their evidence – but once you get the 'further letter', you'd better lodge an appeal: put up or shut up. Even after the appeal has been lodged, you can ask the tribunal to postpone a hearing so that you can round up more evidence or witnesses. Any such extension is at the discretion of the tribunal.

Out of time

The fact that you are too late to lodge an appeal need not be the end of things. You can ask the tribunal to consider an 'appeal out of time': whether they do or not is entirely a matter for the tribunal itself. And you'd better have a good excuse for being late!

Conditions

For an appeal against an amount of tax, the tax must have been paid before the appeal can be heard, unless Customs and Excise (*not* the tribunal) have allowed you not to pay the tax on grounds of hardship. For an appeal against penalty or interest, the appeal can be heard without penalty or interest having been paid. All your VAT returns must be up to date.

After the tribunal

Either side can appeal against the tribunal's decision by going to a higher court, i.e. District Court, High Court, Court of Appeal, House of Lords. Which is where things can get expensive! The VAT tribunal itself charges no fees, of course, and you can conduct your own case if you want to. Or engage lawyers, in which case, you will be responsible for your own expenses, although, if you win, you can ask for costs, just as in any other court.

Unlike any other court, you can ask for interest on any tax you paid, or put on deposit, before the appeal was heard and which is now returnable to you. It also cuts the other way! Although Customs and Excise do not normally demand costs unless the case is very big. They may ask for security to protect the revenue and interest on unpaid tax if they win. The awarding of costs in the higher courts follows normal practice. If matters have got to this pass, get the tribunal notice and do follow the instructions to the letter: you don't want your appeal to fail through some silly procedural slip-up.

Official powers

Too many people 'know their rights', without being able to quote one of them! The Vatman, though, has to know his rights and powers under the relevant legislation – which is, in the main, the VAT Act 1983, plus some amendments from subsequent Finance Acts (the Budget), and the Customs and Excise Management Act 1979. The parts which affect VAT traders are as follow. The Vatman has the power to:

- Require the production of information and documents.
- Inspect records and take extracts.
- Require the production of records from a third party (e.g. from your accountant).
- Require the production of final (annual) accounts (any annual accounts – not just the published ones).
- Enter premises where business is being conducted, or where there is reason to believe business is being conducted, at a reasonable time.

- Inspect the premises.
- Copy records.
- Remove records.
- Take samples.
- Open a gaming machine.
- Require access to, inspect and check any computer and ancilliary equipment or material.
- Make an assessment.

As already mentioned, if fraud or some other crime has been committed, the investigation branch can break in at any time. It is to be hoped that you never experience anything other than a routine visit.

Assessments, penalties and interest

The Vatman has had the power to make assessments ever since VAT began, and they fall into two classes:

1. **Central assessments**, issued from the computer at Southend when returns have not been submitted.

2. **Local assessments**, when a visiting Vatman finds errors in the accounts. These can cover two cases: (*a*) where output tax has not been charged, and (*b*) where input tax has been claimed to which you are not entitled, either because it was specifically not deductible (e.g. on a car) or because you were not entitled for some other reason (e.g. partial exemption or personal use).

Criminal offences and the 'Keith penalties'

Until April 1985, all VAT offences were criminal offences, but in that year's Budget, the 'Keith penalties' were introduced. Lord Keith was chairman of a committee which considered the powers of Inland Revenue and Customs and Excise, and decided that most offences should become civil offences with fixed monetary penalties. Fraud is still a criminal offence, of course, under the Theft Act 1973, but things have got to have reached a pretty serious stage before that Act is invoked.

'Keith' has been introduced in three stages (I wonder what some future researcher will make of that section of VAT lore (and law) labelled 'Keith'? For everything to do with the penalties is known by the noble Lord's name – I suppose it's one way of achieving immortal fame!).

- **Stage 1: Registration**. (See Chapter 2 for registration details and the time limits for compulsory registration.) When first introduced, the penalty for late registration was 30 per cent of the net tax due over the number of days you were late in notifying. It is now 10 per cent up to nine months late, 20 per cent up to 18 months late and 30 per cent over 18 months, subject to a minimum of £50. Also introduced were penalties for failing to notify changes in registered particulars – generally £5 a day.
- **Stage 2: Returns**. The penalty is 5 per cent of the tax due on the first late return, increasing by stages of 5 per cent to a maximum of 30 per cent for subsequent late returns, subject to a minimum of £30. Also, central assessments can be inflated at 20 per cent per period, up to a maximum of 100 per cent, *plus* the penalty for late returns.
- **Stage 3: Payment**

From April 1990, in addition to the penalties, interest has started to be charged on any sum of tax outstanding. At the same time, three other items have been introduced: 1. Serious Misdeclaration Penalty (SMP): 30 per cent of missing tax; 2. Persistent Misdeclaration Penalty: 15 per cent of missing tax; 3. True Tax.

8

Serious misdeclaration

The Keith Committee's designation of 'gross negligence' was softened to 'serious misdeclaration'. It is obvious what their thinking was: the trader who was pretty careless in his bookkeeping. At the same time, a baseline had to be established on which to calculate a serious misdeclaration, and this is the concept of 'true tax'. Obviously, the true tax for any period is the exact amount of tax due or repayable: output tax minus input tax. The misdeclaration becomes serious and you will incur a penalty where, up to a true tax figure of £33,333, a visiting Vatman finds that you have withheld: 30 per cent of the figure (30% of £33,333 = £10,000); or for a true tax figure above £33,333, £10,000 and 5 per cent of the true tax, whichever is the greater; OR that you have accepted and paid an assessment which is less than the true tax by one of the above figures. For example, if the true tax is £80,000 and you withhold £12,000 (i.e. 15 per cent), since £12,000 is less than 30 per cent but is greater than £10,000 and greater than 5 per cent, a penalty is chargeable.

   Indeed, if the true tax is only £100 and you withhold £30, you have committed a serious misdeclaration! This may seem very unfair to the small trader who makes a simple mistake, but it does illustrate the Keith Committee's thoughts about careless bookkeeping. Remember; every £100 of VAT represents nearly £700 of business – and that is quite a 'mistake'!

However, once SMP has been calculated, it's not the end! Consider: you have declared too little tax; the true tax will be the tax already declared *plus* the error (underdeclaration) discovered at a later date. However, if further errors are found later still, then the true tax figure will change and the SMP might be cancelled, because the underdeclaration may then work out at less than 30 per cent. Don't forget that errors can occur on both sides of books! It is clearly in your own interests to keep accurate records: even if an SMP is later cancelled, it can hurt to have to pay it in the first place.

Voluntary disclosure

A serious misdeclaration can conceivably happen by accident and when you recover from the heart attack brought on by the discovery, you will wonder whether you can get out of paying the penalty. The answer is: to some extent. If you find an error in your tax figures amounting to a net £1,000 maximum, you may put it in your current VAT account, add it to the current tax figure and call the resulting total the true tax for the period. Nothing more will be said, even when a visiting Vatman comes across it. But once added in, it must stay. For errors over £1,000, you can avoid the 30 per cent penalty only by telling your LVO before the Vatman's visit. You will still be charged interest, but not the penalty. Either just write with full details, or ask for a Form VAT 652. You will have to give details of the net error in each period.

If you do not volunteer the information until the Vatman phones up for an appointment . . . it's too late! The disclosure must be made at a time when you have no reason to believe that the Vatman is about to take an interest in you. (See Leaflets 700/42, 43.)

Persistent misdeclaration

You don't get much of a chance here: if you underdeclare or overclaim more than £100 or 1 per cent of the true tax twice in two years, you will be assessed for a penalty of 15 per cent of the tax misdeclared. Plus interest, of course. (See Leaflet 700/40.)

Before going further, the difference between a *penalty*, a *surcharge* and *interest* should be made clear:

- A penalty is a fixed 'fine' for a specific offence, expressed either as a percentage of the tax due, or as a fixed sum for a non-tax offence.
- A surcharge is levied on late payment of tax properly due (e.g. late returns).
- Interest is levied on any amount of oustanding tax.

Thus, for a late return, the total payment would be the tax due, *plus* a surcharge of 5 per cent of the tax due, *plus* interest on the tax for the number of days it is withheld. On an assessment, the payment would be the assessed tax plus interest for the number of days since it should have been paid.

The various penalties, surcharges and interest may be summarised as follows:

Offence	Penalty and/or interest
Civil evasion (falling short of criminal fraud).	100 per cent of the missing tax, interest at a daily rate.
Serious misdeclaration (falling short of civil evasion).	30 per cent of the missing tax, interest at a daily rate.
Persistent misdeclaration.	15 per cent of the tax withheld, interest at a daily rate.
Late return.	5–30 per cent of the tax withheld, interest at a daily rate.
Local assessment.	30 per cent penalty if 'serious', interest at a daily rate.
Failure to notify for: - registration. - change in supplies (when exempted from registration).	10–30 per cent of the net tax for number of days late (or £50 whichever is greater), interest at a daily rate.
Issue of tax invoices by an unregistered person.	30 per cent of the tax, plus the tax, interest at a daily rate.
Breach of walking possession[1].	50 per cent of tax involved.
Failure to: - notify end of trading. - keep or produce records. - observe other regulations[2].	£5 a day while the failure continues; £10 for second offences; £15 for third offences; minimum penalty £50. Penalty runs for a maximum of 100 days.
Failure to preserve records for 6 years.	£500

8

[1] 'Walking possession' means that a bailiff has seized some of your goods, but has not removed them from your premises. You may not sell those goods, or remove them, until the possession is lifted. If you do, the penalty is half the tax for which the goods were seized in the first place.

[2] The other regulatory offences are failure to:
- sign VAT 1.
- notify partners on VAT 2.
- notify change in registration details.
- notify death or incapacity of registered person.
- issue tax invoice in time.
- issue a complete tax invoice.
- identify different rates on a tax invoice.
- supply credit note in time after rate change.
- issue tax invoice by retailer.
- adjust provisional partial exemption inputs.
- use special method for two years.
- show VAT number on postal import declaration.
- observe temporary import conditions.
- furnish a final VAT return.
- furnish auction statement for taxable person.
- account for all tax due on a return.
- adjust estimated output tax.
- provide evidence for input tax.
- adjust estimated input tax.
- correct errors in a return.

For intending traders, failure to:
- refund tax repaid if business does not start.
- keep invoices.
- keep records of a building or site.
- notify one no longer intends to make supplies.

On bad debts, failure to:
- preserve evidence
- repay incorrect claim

For retailers, failure to observe requirements in Notice 727 and supplements.

Local assessments

With the new regulations introduced in April 1990, a visiting Vatman is no longer able to issue a local assessment directly: he must notify the Southend HQ where the figures will be fed through the number-cruncher to calculate the intererst *week by week* since the offence was committed, and then issue an assessment, plus interest and penalty. For instance, suppose you omitted the motoring scale charge; the Vatman will notify his HQ of the specific tax periods in which the omission occurred, and the number-cruncher will work out the interest due on each period's missing scale charge, from the end of the period to the date of discovery.

Central assessments

Much the same applies to central assessments/missing returns: once the tax due in each period has been established, interest will be calculated for each period up to the time the true tax figure is established.

How much interest?

The rate of interest is set by the Treasury, week by week, to reflect the commercial rate of interest chargeable on borrowed funds/overdrafts, etc. It is applied at simple rate, not compound, and is not charged on penalties.

How far back can they go?

Practically as far as they like – up to 20 years. But not earlier than April 1990: at least British law has never gone in for retrospective legislation. So your withheld tax will be interest-free up to April 1990. (But not penalty-free!)

Appeals and 'reasonable excuse'

All penalties, surcharges and interest are appealable, but only on the grounds of 'reasonable excuse'. Simple ignorance of the law is never taken as an excuse in any system, especially if the knowledge is published, and lack of funds to pay the tax is certainly not a 'reasonable' excuse. Nor is the fact that you relied on someone else and they let you down: it is the registered person who is entirely responsible for conducting his VAT affairs in compliance with the law. So what is a 'reasonable excuse'? There is no legally defined, universal excuse – each case will be treated on its merits. Certainly, illness is a reasonable enough excuse, provided you can prove it, or a family emergency (e.g. death, sudden illness, an accident to the children, etc.), and, of course, any specific misdirection by an officer of Customs and Excise, or 'misdirection by omission' – something so obvious that it should have been brought to your attention but wasn't, so you could only assume that it was OK. For instance, a trader had a three-day visit from a senior officer, accompanied by an officer on two days, who OKed the books. A year later, another officer walked in and the first thing he noticed was that one column in the cash-book was always one line longer than all the rest: it simply could not be missed. It turned out that the trader conducted 'shop within shop' operations: all but one of the stores charged him 'rent' as a percentage of his tax-exclusive sales; the odd one charged a percentage of the tax-inclusive sales. He thought that this meant that the store was accounting for 20 per cent of his output tax, so that extra line in the one column was where he reduced his output tax by 20 per cent. All in all, it came down to the fact that he had been misled by omission, and a deputy commissioner wrote off some £9,000 tax. But be warned: it is the Vatman's intention, once the serious misdeclaration penalty is in force, that misdirection by omission will no longer be a reasonable excuse, especially since a tax period, once inspected and 'passed', can be re-inspected for further errors. In my opinion, if a visiting Vatman is so careless as to overlook obvious errors and fails to draw them to your attention, you should still have a reasonable excuse when a second Vatman finds his predecessor's mistake.

I hope this gives some idea of what may be accepted as a reasonable excuse – it cannot be defined any more closely. So – if you are caught by one of the Vatman's penalties – think up a good excuse and try it out! It should however be pointed out that although all these penalties exist, they are not imposed on every occasion. Even the Vatman recognises that people make mistakes, or may not be aware of the requirement until it is specifically pointed out to them. The penalties are imposed only for persistent offenders as a rule, or in cases of blatant flouting of the law and regulations, or where a lot of tax is involved. And usually, a fair warning is given first. Take the case of a late return. Everyone may be late with a return for various reasons. So a first late return is merely recorded in the Vatman's computer. A second late return within 12 months brings forth a warning letter – a 'surcharge liability notice' – which says that, if there is another late return within 12 months, the penalty will be imposed and, for every late return thereafter, there will be a 'surcharge liability extension notice', which will remain in effect until there are four consecutive returns submitted on time.

Furthermore, for most of these crimes, the local Vatman has to persuade his HQ to start the penalty system, and if they don't think the crime is serious enough, they won't do it. These penalties are there for the Vatman to clobber the rogue, the regular fiddler, the sort of person who never pays a bill till he gets the red demand – on the grounds that his money is sitting in a bank, earning interest. But the occasional offender will normally only get a warning. So sleep easy.

Selling to official bodies

There is really very little to say here: you deal with officialdom (for business/VAT purposes) exactly as you deal with any other registered trader. Oh, yes – they are all registered for VAT!

Local authorities are registered in the ordinary series: 123 4567 89. You charge them VAT as appropriate, and if you buy business supplies from them, (i.e. anything from annual rent of an off-street parking space to scrap furniture and the like) they must give you a tax invoice. How can you tell if it is a 'business supply'? Ask yourself: is this the sort of supply I could get from any other trader? If the answer is 'Yes', and you haven't got a tax invoice, ask for one. If a tax invoice is refused, contact your LVO and ask for a ruling: there is no reason why you should be deprived of input tax simply because some local authority clerk doesn't know anything about VAT.

Government departments have a special VAT number: GD followed by three figures, starting at 001. Once again, you make supplies to them in exactly the same way as to any other peson – with VAT. There are no circumstances where VAT is not charged, except under the new building regulations in which case, they must give you a certificate of entitlement to zero-rating.

Military purchasing and local purchasing officers, already mentioned, delight in getting rubber stamps made and plastering them all over local traders' invoices, to the effect that 'We don't pay VAT'. So tell them three things:

1. That they have no authority to refuse to pay VAT and that they are therefore acting outside their authority and that you will sue them personally, in their private capacity, for the VAT.
2. That they should refer to MOD's own internal instructions on VAT.
3. That you will report the matter fully, in writing, to your LVO, and will ask them to report the matter to VAH2 at VAT headquarters. And tell the LVO that, if you are assessed for the VAT the MOD refuses to pay to you, you will immediately report the matter to your MP and the VAT tribunal. (The LVO must also provide you with tribunal appeal notices and forms. On demand.)

The same procedure applies to any other government department, although MOD is by far the worst. Health authorities also have a special registration: HA followed by three numbers, and everything

said about government departments applies equally to them.
Remember this:

- VAT is charged on a supply made by you.
- There is no one who doesn't pay VAT.
- Under certain conditions, normally standard rate supplies can be supplied at zero rate (see Chapter 3).

I hope that I have been able to smooth out a few problems for you in these pages. And remember, the best way to keep the Vatman off your back is . . . do it right, first time! Best of luck.

Appendix:
Budget 1990 changes

Registration limit

Turnover limit for registration has been increased to £25,400 per year, and quarterly figures are no longer required.

Gradual build-up

The same conditions still apply, except that only the annual turnover figure now applies. For example, have you exceeded the limit *in the past 12 calendar months?* You will have to examine your turnover month by month, regardless of calendar quarters or financial year, and notify within 30 days of the end of any month in which you exceed the annual limit.

Seasonal trade

Quarterly figures no longer apply, so if you never reach the annual figure, there is no need to notify. However, if there are factors which cause an annual fluctuation – like the Bed & Breakfast operator – you must still notify and argue for exemption from registration afterwards.

Take-over

Treat the previous owner's turnover in the past 12 months as your own: remember, you are taking over a *going concern* (which is already registered, or is above the registration limit in its own right) and carrying on as though there had been no change of ownership. You will not be allowed a 'free year' on a business which is already proven to be over the limit.

Future success

You are no longer required to register because you believe that you *expect* to turn over more than the registration limit in the *next* 12 months. However, setting up a business will still be expensive and if you want to recover input tax as you go along, you can still register as an intending trader or voluntarily. Write to your LVO explaining why you want to be registered in advance of trading.

Yo-yo

See 'Seasonal trade' above. There could still be factors which affect your business year by year: the same conditions on remaining registered still apply.

Bad debts

There is no longer any need to prove that the bad debtor is bankrupt, in liquidation, etc. – just wait until the debt is two years old. It will probably be getting on that way anyway by the time you've tried all means of getting your money. But still do not be tempted to cancel a bad debt by issuing a credit note: the Vatman will still raise an assessment and interest for the period during which the tax was still owing. Wait the two years and get it free: just show, in your annual accounts, that the bad debt has been written off and enter the VAT in the VAT account. (See p. 62, C3)

Index